Stop Smoking
NOW!

The rewarding journey to a smoke-free life

A CLEVELAND CLINIC GUIDE

Garland Y. DeNelsky, Ph.D.

Cleveland Clinic Press

Cleveland, Ohio

Stop Smoking Now!
The rewarding journey to a smoke-free life
A CLEVELAND CLINIC GUIDE

Cleveland Clinic Press
All rights reserved
Copyright © 2007 Cleveland Clinic

Contact:
Cleveland Clinic Press • 9500 Euclid Ave. NA32
Cleveland, OH 44195
216-445-5547
delongk@ccf.org
www.clevelandclinicpress.org

This book is not intended to replace personal medical care and supervision; there is no substitute for the experience and information that your doctor can provide. Rather, it is our hope that this book will provide additional information to help people understand the nature of tobacco use and addiction.

Proper medical care always should be tailored to the individual patient. If you read something in this book that seems to conflict with your doctor's instructions, contact your doctor. Since each case is different, there will be good reasons for individual treatment to differ from the information presented in this book.

If you have any questions about any treatment in this book, consult your doctor.

The patient names and cases used in this book are composite cases drawn from several sources.

Library of Congress Cataloging-in-Publication Data
DeNelsky, Garland Y., 1938-
Stop Smoking Now! A Cleveland Clinic Guide / Garland Y. DeNelsky
p. cm.
Includes index.
ISBN 978-1-59624-051-3 (alk. paper)
1. Smoking cessation. 2.Nicotine addiction – Treatment.
3. Cigarette smokers – Rehabilitation. 4. Tobacco use. I. Title.
RC567.D46 2007   616.86'506–dc22
2007006728

Book Design by Whitney Campbell
Illustrations by Joe Kanasz and Ken Kula, Cleveland Clinic Department of Medical Illustration

Acknowledgments

I wish to express my appreciation to several individuals who expertly contributed to this effort, including publisher Dr. John Clough, editors Kathryn DeLong, Benjamin Gleisser, and Julianne Stein, and artists Joe Kanasz and Ken Kula. Special gratitude is owed to my wife, Ellen, who not only supported my efforts but also provided valuable feedback and served as a skillful proofreader. Thanks are also due to my colleague and friend Betty Lewine, who encouraged me to write this book years ago, even before I owned a computer!

I am also enormously grateful to those wonderful people in my life who encouraged me to quit smoking many years ago. Without their patient support I probably would not have been around to undertake this project. Finally, I wish to thank the many thousands of smokers with whom I have had the privilege to work this past quarter-century. Being able to accompany you on your journeys toward a tobacco-free life has been enlightening and inspirational.

Contents

Preface

If I hadn't quit smoking, I might not be alive today. In fact, quitting smoking is the one accomplishment in my life of which I am proudest.

I'm also proud of my role in helping thousands of others achieve healthier lives. My passion for smoking cessation was the driving force behind my founding the Cleveland Clinic's Smoking Cessation Program and serving as its director for more than twenty years. Over that time, I saw thousands of smokers struggle to overcome their tobacco dependency and applauded each of their triumphs. Today it is wonderfully exhilarating to meet ex-smokers long after they've quit and hear them talk about their journey to a smoke-free life in positive, even glowing terms. They love how their lives have improved. They're proud of their success and happy to be alive. They're inspirational.

But let me tell you something interesting I've noticed. After years of helping people quit smoking, I concluded that smokers who were preparing to quit looked upon the road ahead of them as dismal, forbidding, and even frightening. Most approached their quit day with considerable dread, almost as though they were about to embark on a terrible trip that they had to take (but dearly wished they didn't have to). Nearly all had doubts about whether they could stay with the quitting process. Even those who were highly committed to quitting were grim, almost as though they were about to march off to their own execution!

This bleak picture of those who are afraid to quit stands in stark contrast to those who have successfully quit. Months – even years – after they quit, whenever I encountered them, they thanked me for my help and told me how wonderful they felt now that they were no longer smoking. At times, their mood was joyful as they cheerfully related the difficulties they had faced and the obstacles they overcame to remain smoke-free. They sounded like mountain climbers boasting of conquering a forbidding peak.

Evident in their narratives was the pride they felt in themselves. They remembered (and often celebrated!) the anniversary of their quitting dates. I cannot count the number of times I heard this statement: "Quitting was the best thing I ever did for myself!"

What had started out as a grim mission for these people had become, in retrospect, a splendid, life-affirming journey.

Yet, here was what I couldn't understand: If quitting smoking was such an upbeat experience, why did some people still cling to their tobacco addiction?

Gradually, I began to understand that some smokers who contemplate quitting see the road to a smoke-free life as a long, arduous trip with an end that may not be clearly in sight. Certainly, they know the destination is a reward worth achieving, but the journey contains challenges and obstacles in the form of bumps along the path, detours to be negotiated, and even hardships to be endured.

But difficult does not mean impossible. Millions of people have quit.

And so can you.

When people decide to take a major trip, they must commit not only to the journey but to all the obstacles, setbacks, and disappointments that come along with it. So it is with quitting smoking. There are, of course, techniques such as behavior therapy, nicotine replacement, medications, group support, hypnosis, and other practices that may make the road a little smoother and the obstacles less difficult. (We will discuss these techniques and many others in this book.) But there is no method or magic pill available now – or likely to be available in the future – that will take the place of a firm and unwavering commitment to the goal of a smoke-free life. Just as a determined traveler who sets out for California is not going to turn back because of an automobile breakdown or a major detour, neither is a determined quitter going to go back to smoking because of a strong urge to smoke or a major crisis in his or her life.

I feel a great deal of passion for this topic, which I hope will shine through in these pages. Major driving forces behind this passion are my own experiences and the experiences of others. After twenty-four years of smoking, two bouts of pneumonia, and several unsuccessful attempts at quitting, I quit tobacco more than a quarter of a century ago. If I were still smoking and still alive, there is no doubt that my quality of life would have been seriously jeopardized. I would not have the breath or stamina to enjoy playing tennis, go on bicycle rides, take long walks, or simply appreciate the wonderful smells of spring and autumn – and the list goes on and on.

There are so many marvelous benefits of becoming tobacco-free! Without question, quitting smoking was the best gift I ever gave myself. I am very proud of myself for having quit and for staying smoke-free. Every deep breath I take reminds me of this.

And if I can do it, so can you.

Garland Y. DeNelsky, Ph.D.

Chapter 1

The Power of the Addiction – the Journey to Freedom

Brian knew very well that what he was doing was wrong as well as downright idiotic. But the urge was overpowering.

He secured his hospital gown as best he could, cleared a path for his IV pole, and cautiously walked down the hallway toward the stairs. Pain from the incision in his chest reminded him, while he was walking, that he had had heart surgery only nine days earlier. And with that reminder came the memory of the admonitions of his cardiologist, his heart surgeon, and all the other doctors and nurses who had spoken with him during his hospital stay. If he wanted his open-heart surgery to be successful, and if he wanted to live to see his children become adults and his grandchildren born, *he must quit smoking.*

He totally agreed with his doctors; he knew the dangers of smoking. So why, then, was he doing this?

He soon realized that walking down six flights of stairs to the lobby to get outside was nearly out of the question. His IV pole was heavy and clumsy to maneuver, and he wasn't strong enough to slide it down the numerous steps he'd have to traverse. Taking the elevator also proved out of the question, as it was nearly fully loaded with doctors and nurses every time it stopped at his floor. Besides, patients were never supposed to leave the floor by themselves, especially with an IV in tow.

But he *had* to get to the ground. He just *had* to go outside for a cigarette.

Somehow, some way, Brian managed to get down those six flights of stairs with his IV pole. He felt a mixture of pain, guilt, and excitement – especially on the next to last flight of stairs, when his pole slipped and he nearly fell trying to catch it. But soon he was at the door leading outside. And even though it was a chilly day in early spring, and he was wearing only his hospital gown, he shoved open the door.

A sharp stab of pain from the wound on his chest sliced through him as he raised his right hand to light his cigarette. At that moment, the door slammed shut behind him, leaving him alone in an area of the hospital grounds that was obviously not meant for patients to visit. After taking three long drags from his cigarette – which made him unbelievably dizzy and light-headed – he slowly reached back to see whether the door behind him would open.

It would not.

He was trapped somewhere in the back of the hospital with nothing except his hospital gown, his IV pole, and his lit cigarette! But there was nothing to worry about. He was midway through the cigarette and having that "special feeling" – often termed a "buzz" – that he'd experienced thousands of times before. At some level he understood what drove his seemingly bizarre behavior and led him to the place he was now.

He knew he was going to be in trouble with the nurses and doctors. He also knew that his body was going to be in trouble because he was smoking again. It had been more than two weeks since his last cigarette, and he'd hardly missed them. But the craving to "have one" had started when one of his smoking friends visited him earlier in the day. It got worse when he received a call from his office reminding him of a special project he needed to start as soon as he returned to work. And it seemed insurmountable after his wife called him with the news that their water heater had broken and their basement was flooding.

He finished his first cigarette amazingly quickly. By the end of it, he wasn't feeling woozy anymore. He knew that somehow he'd have to find the front door of the hospital and negotiate his way back to his room. And he knew that what he faced wasn't going to be pleasant – a patient fresh from heart surgery disobeying orders and leaving the building to have a cigarette! How was he going to explain himself? He needed a little time to think, to plan. So he pulled out a second cigarette and lit it only moments after finishing his first.

Somehow, Brian managed to find the door labeled "Hospital Admitting." By the time he found it – perhaps fifteen minutes after he began his search – he was cold and in considerable pain, and he wanted another smoke. He'd asked a few astonished persons along the way for directions and had received some very strange looks and a couple of sarcastic comments. He tried to look casual as he strode with his IV pole and hospital gown into the admitting lobby. But it didn't work; several admitting personnel surrounded him immediately, astonished and annoyed that he'd left his floor, dragged his IV pole down six flights of stairs, and risked his health – indeed, his life – to enjoy a couple of cigarettes. He knew he'd hear plenty about his behavior later from all the hospital folks who worked with him daily. And, of course, he did.

Brian wasn't an especially rebellious person, and he certainly wasn't a habitual rule-breaker. He was 41, married, and a father of three, employed as a computer systems specialist, and active in his community and church. But since the age of 15, he'd been hooked on nicotine, that ingredient in tobacco that keeps people coming back for more and more – coming back even though they know all the health risks and desperately want to do otherwise. Brian knew how easily one gets re-hooked on smoking, even after a long interlude without tobacco. After all, he'd quit several times in his life – once for nearly two years – but always, in a moment of weakness, he had lit up again. Within a few days, he was back to smoking as though he'd never quit.

Brian's story is not unusual, even though his getting trapped outside with a hospital gown and an IV pole is. Surveys show that a strong majority of smokers (about 90 percent) would quit smoking if they could. Even people with health problems caused by smoking, such as lung cancer, emphysema, or heart disease – people who both need to and want to quit – have to struggle to rid themselves of the nicotine "monkey on their back." And even the ones who are courageous enough to quit must remain vigilant for many years to ensure that they don't slide backward in an unguarded moment and get re-hooked.

It has been said that the essence of addiction is our inability to regulate our behavior, despite a strong desire to do so and a clear understanding of the bad things that will happen to us if we don't.

Many experts believe that nicotine is one of the most powerfully addictive substances in the world. People get hooked on smoking more easily than on almost any other addiction; one study reported that smoking only a couple of cigarettes completely is enough to hook most kids. Smoking is also the most overindulged addiction in the world. What alcoholic will have twenty, thirty, forty, or more drinks a day for thirty or forty years? What heroin addict has one "hit" upon arising each morning, another while driving to work, more during coffee breaks, and several more later while watching television in the evening? Or when boredom, fear, and dozens of other triggers present themselves several times each day? Indeed, it's a wonder that people are able to quit smoking (or stop using any form of tobacco) at all.

Despite all the reasons that nicotine is such a powerful, deeply ingrained addiction, and in spite of the struggle required for smokers to free themselves from this dangerous behavior, people do quit. **More than 46 million Americans have quit smoking forever.** Indeed, this is one of the most monumental revolutions in behavior ever to occur in this country.

Quitting smoking involves inconvenience and difficulty, but the rewards and satisfactions of living a tobacco-free life make the difficulty worth it. Not only can ex-smokers count on improved health, increased life expectancy, and enhanced vigor; they also experience improved feelings of self-worth. To put it another way, ex-smokers not only feel better physically; they feel better about themselves.

The purpose of this book is to be a guide for what can be one of the most rewarding journeys a person can make – the journey to a smoke-free life. This guide is meant not only for smokers, but also for those who are involved with and concerned about a smoker's welfare, and want to be helpful in the right way.

Quitting smoking may be a challenging journey for some, but virtually all who have completed it are delighted and thankful.

Chapter 2

Why Quit?

Michelle seemed younger than the "typical" smoker who wants to quit. She was in her early 30s, attractive and athletic, and was dressed quite casually in a tennis warm-up outfit. Yet there was a sadness and an anxiousness about her. She'd been referred to me for help with quitting smoking, and early in our interview, she revealed that she was an avid tennis player who'd competed in both high school and college, and now played club tennis at a relatively high level.

But all this was about to change. She could no longer play tennis; indeed, her life was undergoing dramatic changes and all her plans were in doubt.

A few weeks earlier, while playing tennis, she experienced a dizzy spell unlike anything she'd ever had. At first, she discounted her light-headed-ness, speculating that it was stress-related. After all, she was married and had three young children as well as a challenging job and a very active lifestyle. But when the dizzy spells worsened, she saw her doctor. He imme-diately referred her to a neurologist, who discovered a malignant brain tumor. Further tests revealed that her brain cancer was not the original site of her disease. After only about a dozen years of smoking less than a pack per day, Michelle had lung cancer that had metastasized to her brain.

The prognosis was guarded, if not actually bleak. What in Michelle's life had gone wrong?

The answer was simple: *smoking.*

Although most lung-cancer patients have smoked for twenty or thirty years or more before developing their deadly disease, there are plenty of exceptions. And unlucky Michelle, who did everything "right" to take care of her health (except for smoking), was one of those unfortunate ones. Her lung cancer had developed silently within her, an all-too-common occur-rence. Then, by means of a mechanism similar to the lung-brain connection that so quickly and efficiently delivers nicotine to the brain, the lung cancer migrated to her brain. Sadly, as Michelle learned, smokers don't have to smoke for decades and decades to experience the devastating consequences of their deadly behavior.

Quantity of life

Tobacco affects virtually every organ of the body. Lung cancer, which is the single most deadly disease attributable to smoking, takes the lives of more than 123,000 people in the United States every year. More than 85 percent of all lung-cancer deaths are attributable to smoking. Taking second place in this deadly sweepstakes is coronary heart disease: Smoking causes about 100,000 coronary heart disease deaths each year. In third place are chronic obstructive lung diseases, of which emphysema is the most common. In fact, the United States' top doctor – the Surgeon General – estimates that smoking causes more than 90 percent of all chronic obstructive lung disease deaths.

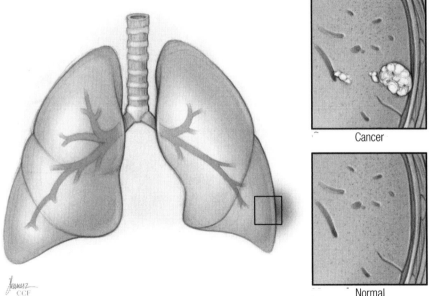

Cancer

Normal

Smoking is responsible for many other kinds of death as well. Various reports from the Surgeon General have concluded that smoking is a major cause of strokes, of which there are more than 600,000 yearly in the United States. Smoking also produces cancer in numerous organs of the body. Starting from the head and moving toward the feet, smoking is behind cancers of the mouth, throat, larynx, esophagus, lungs, stomach, pancreas, kidney, bladder (see illustration at left), and for women, the cervix. And smoking causes abdominal aortic aneurysm, a bulge in the wall of the aorta near the stomach; each year, about 15,000 Americans die from this condition. Women who smoke while pregnant have a higher risk of premature rupture of membranes before labor begins. This can lead to premature birth and possibly infant death. And here is a fact: Nonsmokers have healthier babies.

Since smoking is so overwhelmingly poisonous to nearly every organ of the body, it's easy to become desensitized to the seemingly endless parade of statistics that can be marshaled against it. (Of course, as Michelle demonstrated, the statistics become intensely vivid, personal, and impossible to ignore once an individual has been diagnosed with one of the deadly diseases caused by smoking.)

Consider these findings from the Surgeon General's 2004 Report "The Health Consequences of Smoking on the Human Body":

1. Smoking harms nearly every organ of your body, causing many diseases that negatively affect your health.

2. Quitting smoking has immediate and long-term benefits, reduces risks for diseases caused by smoking, and improves your health in general.

3. Smoking cigarettes with lower tar and nicotine provides no clear benefit to health.

4. The list of diseases caused by smoking has been expanded to include acute myeloid leukemia, cataracts, pneumonia, and periodontitis.

In short, tobacco is the most deadly product ever developed by humanity. In the past 200 years, it has slain more people than all the wars, drugs, auto accidents, homicides, and suicides *put together*. It's the only consumer product that produces illness and death when *used as directed*. Smoking kills, on average, about 430,000 Americans each year. This breaks down to more than 1,170 deaths each day.

To put this into perspective, the horrific events of September 11, 2001, claimed approximately 3,020 lives. How long does it take smoking to claim the lives of this many Americans? Less than three days!

Several studies have demonstrated that on average, cigarette smokers die between ten and fourteen years sooner than nonsmokers. While the life expectancy of nonsmokers has been increasing steadily since 1900, the lifespan of smokers has been progressively decreasing. In addition to these years of lost life, smokers tend to become ill and disabled for even more years, further detracting from their years of healthy life.

Tobacco smoke: A most deadly cocktail

Why is smoking so dangerous? Tobacco smoke contains more than 4,000 different chemicals, many of which are known poisons. More than fifty of

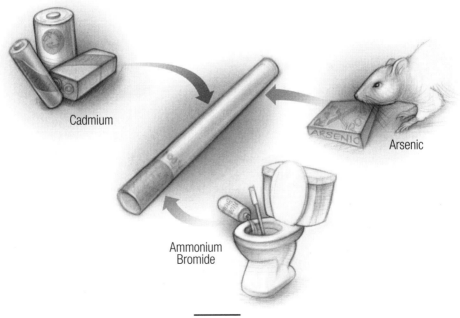

Cadmium

Arsenic

Ammonium Bromide

these chemicals are known to cause cancer in humans. Everyone knows that tobacco contains nicotine, but many aren't aware that nicotine is a potent nerve poison and is included in many insecticides. Nicotine in the bloodstream also increases the LDL ("bad") cholesterol, which can clog and harden arteries and boost the risk of heart attack and stroke.

Tobacco smoke also contains carbon monoxide, the deadly, colorless, odorless gas that is produced as a result of incomplete combustion. Exposure to carbon monoxide reduces the blood's ability to carry oxygen, so the muscles – including the heart – get less oxygen. This requires the heart to work harder. Carbon monoxide is also known to cause microscopic lesions on the smooth inner surface of blood vessels – lesions that contribute to cardiovascular disease and other circulatory disorders.

The list of deadly compounds in tobacco smoke also includes ammonium bromide (a toilet cleaner), benzene (an industrial solvent), arsenic (a rat poison), cadmium (used in rechargeable batteries), cyanide (a poison used in gas chambers), formaldehyde (used to embalm bodies), lead (a poison now removed from nearly all paints), mercury (highly poisonous and easily absorbed through the respiratory tract), nickel (a carcinogen), and many other known toxic substances. It's hard to imagine a more deadly cocktail of poisons than that contained in tobacco smoke!

Quality of life

Tobacco's devastating impact on health is more than sufficient reason to quit. Not only does smoking destroy health and shorten lives, but it also has a very negative impact on a person's *quality* of life. June's story is an example of how this can occur.

June was a young woman in her mid-20s when she came for assistance in quitting smoking. Her opening statement was both powerful and unusual: "I have to either quit smoking or break my engagement!"

In about a month, June was scheduled to travel with her fiancé to meet his parents and stay with them for a long weekend. They were adamantly against smoking, and she didn't wish to displease them. The weekend with his parents was so tightly scheduled that she foresaw no opportunity to sneak a cigarette now and then. She couldn't imagine being without her cigarettes – in other words, to go without nicotine. Her life was being controlled by her need to light up.

Was June looking for a way out of her engagement and using her need to smoke as an excuse? Exploring their relationship revealed no evidence for this possibility. Her fiancé, Bob, was the finest man she'd ever met, and she knew that she was deeply in love with him and he with her. So compatible were they that she could easily picture the two of them happily married for a lifetime. But as powerful as her feelings for him were, her fear of going several days without smoking seemed equally powerful – so strong, in fact, that she was seriously considering giving up the love of her life for the nicotine in her cigarettes!

Thankfully, June's story had a very happy ending. She *did* quit smoking before the trip to meet her future in-laws, had a wonderful weekend visit, and eventually married Bob. Several years later, while pregnant, she related that she couldn't believe she had seriously considered giving up what turned out to be a wonderful marriage in order to keep smoking! She was healthy, happy with her life, and delighted with her status as a nonsmoker.

June's story illustrates one of the most powerful benefits of quitting smoking: *Nicotine no longer controls your life.* To a significant degree, the need to smoke does control your life. As a smoker, you're constantly planning where you'll go (or not go) and whom you'll be with (or not with) in order to regularly satisfy your need for nicotine. In many places, you feel as though you're treated as an outcast because you smoke – and you're constantly being urged to quit.

If you're like most smokers, smoking regulates many aspects of your life, from the time you arise in the morning to when you retire to bed at night. In the back of your mind, you worry about the damage your smoking is doing to your body. In many ways, nicotine can be likened to a highly controlling dictator from whom there seems to be no escape. And one of the greatest benefits of quitting is that you're freed from this dictator. Despite the conventional belief that smoking helps people cope with stress, it has been well demonstrated that you'll feel less stress six months after quitting than you did when you were smoking – and one reason for this is that you're no longer controlled by your need for nicotine. You've achieved freedom from your deadly nicotine dictator!

Smoking has a negative effect on quality of life in many, many other ways as well. For example, smoking is the opposite of the "fountain of youth." It ages you prematurely. It produces wrinkles before you'd ordinarily develop

such wrinkles. And in another skin-related development, you're more likely to experience frostbite when exposed to cold air.

Smoking also contributes to infertility problems and causes women to go into menopause earlier. It has been clearly identified as a major cause of impotence in men.

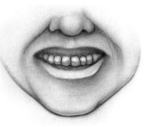

In addition to causing bad breath and stained teeth, smoking delays the healing of gum infections, mouth lesions, and wounds that are caused as a result of dental procedures. Indeed, smoking impedes healing of many types.

Smoking causes infections of the linings of the mucous membranes of the nose, mouth, and lungs, which can cause continuous coughing. As a

smoker, you're more likely to develop pneumonia, bronchitis, and other respiratory problems. You're more likely to develop circulatory problems throughout your body. The list goes on and on; smoking has a negative impact on quality of life in so many ways.

But when you quit smoking, your sense of smell returns. And since your body is no longer being deprived of oxygen and subjected to the multiple poisons in tobacco, you have more energy and vigor.

One of the least recognized improvements involves self-esteem. To quote one ex-smoker, "It's absolutely amazing how your whole outlook on life changes when you quit smoking. Your self-esteem gets so much better and you want to take those feelings and do other healthier things for yourself.

Once you get out of one bad habit, it seems you want to keep going and break other bad habits. At least it has worked that way for me."

It also worked that way for Claudia, a woman in her mid-30s. Claudia came from a difficult early background: Her overly critical parents rarely praised or psychologically nurtured her. When she later visited a psychologist, it was hard for her to describe anything positive about herself. She seemed to have internalized the criticism surrounding her in her early years. She stumbled and hesitated when asked to come up with even one thing she liked about herself, one thing she was proud of.

Then her eyes brightened, and a rare smile slowly spread across her face. "I quit smoking over five years ago and I'm very, very proud of myself for doing that. It's the best thing I've ever done!"

When we value something, whether a shiny new automobile or our own body, we're likely to take care of it. None of us would remove the air filter on our new car and drive it down dusty roads, exposing its inner workings to the ravages of dirty air. Yet you do the same thing to your body many times each day by inhaling the dozens of poisonous chemicals in tobacco smoke! That's why there's no greater gift you can give yourself than quitting smoking. When we give ourselves that gift, we're telling ourselves that we're worth the effort it takes to be healthy. And when we make that effort and become successful nonsmokers, we affirm our own worth. We end up feeling better about ourselves; our self-esteem is enhanced.

Financial costs

Smoking exacts a terrible toll on both quantity (length) and quality of life. And what about financial costs? At the time of this writing, the cost of a pack of cigarettes is about $4.32. At that price, a pack-a-day smoker burns through about $30.24 per week, or nearly $1,600 per year. That's a sizable mortgage payment or a nice vacation with the family. According to *Money Magazine*, a 40-year-old who quits smoking and puts the savings into a 401(k) earning 9 percent a year would have an extra $250,000 by age 70.

And that's only the start: Smokers pay significantly more than nonsmokers for life and health insurance. Smokers receive less money on average when they trade in their cars or sell their houses; the foul-smelling residue from their smoke makes both assets less desirable.

Smoking also places a financial burden on society. According to the American Lung Association, smoking costs over $150 billion each year in excess health-care costs and lost productivity in the United States. Can you believe that some tobacco apologists have argued that part of that is "given back" to society, since smokers die early and hence collect fewer Social Security and Medicare payments!

Recovery from smoking

The benefits from quitting are enormous. Figure 1 illustrates some of them.

First and foremost, when you stop smoking, you greatly reduce your risk of dying prematurely. Smoking cessation also lowers your risk of lung and other types of cancer; your risk of developing cancer declines in ratio to the number of years since you stopped smoking. Coronary heart disease is substantially reduced within one to two years of cessation; after fifteen years of not smoking, your risk of coronary heart disease is the same as that of a nonsmoker. Cessation reduces respiratory symptoms, such as coughing, wheezing, and shortness of breath. Lung function improves when you quit smoking. If you're a woman and you stop smoking before or during pregnancy, you reduce your risk of adverse reproductive outcomes such as infertility or having a low-birth-weight baby.

After ten to fifteen years of abstinence, your risk of dying from any smoking-related disease is nearly as low as that of persons who have never smoked. These facts confirm the conclusion that you can give yourself no gift greater, more valuable, or more lasting than the gift of cessation.

Why quit smoking? To remain healthy and vigorous, to feel good about yourself, to age normally, and to stay alive. These are some mighty powerful reasons to take the journey to a smoke-free life!

Benefits of Quitting

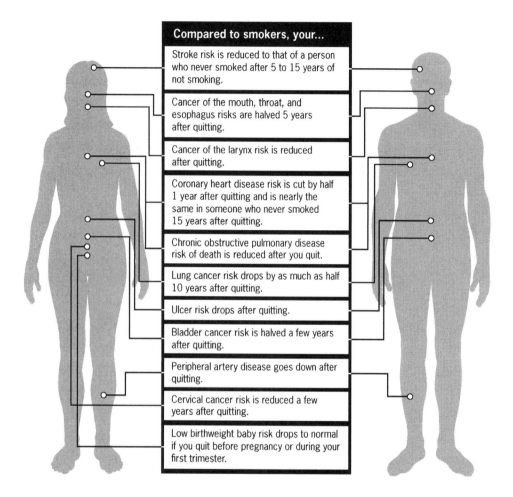

Compared to smokers, your...

Stroke risk is reduced to that of a person who never smoked after 5 to 15 years of not smoking.

Cancer of the mouth, throat, and esophagus risks are halved 5 years after quitting.

Cancer of the larynx risk is reduced after quitting.

Coronary heart disease risk is cut by half 1 year after quitting and is nearly the same in someone who never smoked 15 years after quitting.

Chronic obstructive pulmonary disease risk of death is reduced after you quit.

Lung cancer risk drops by as much as half 10 years after quitting.

Ulcer risk drops after quitting.

Bladder cancer risk is halved a few years after quitting.

Peripheral artery disease goes down after quitting.

Cervical cancer risk is reduced a few years after quitting.

Low birthweight baby risk drops to normal if you quit before pregnancy or during your first trimester.

Figure 1– The benefits of quitting smoking, as reported by the Centers for Disease Control and Prevention

Chapter 3

How Did This Begin Anyway?

Few adolescents report that they actually *planned* to start smoking. When asked, many young smokers say that starting smoking was just something that happened to them, almost like catching a cold or breaking a leg. But a closer look makes it clear that lighting up that first cigarette is no chance event.

Andy had his first smoke at the age of 11. Cigarettes were readily available to him; not only did his father smoke, but so did his 16-year-old brother, Charlie. Andy idolized his older brother. Charlie was popular, a very good student, and an excellent athlete. He didn't encourage Andy to smoke; in fact, Charlie urged Andy to stay away from tobacco – period.

At the age of 15, Charlie had made a sincere effort to quit, hoping to find greater stamina on the basketball court. He was surprised to find out that it was very hard – actually, impossible – for him to go without smoking even for the few months of basketball season. Charlie warned his younger brother that once tobacco "gets hold of you, it's not easy to let go of it, not easy at all! So don't get started!"

Smoking was a longstanding source of strife in Andy's family. Andy's mother, a nonsmoker, was adamantly against smoking – her husband's smoking in particular. Her own mother, who smoked, had died of lung cancer at a relatively early age, and she worried about losing her husband prematurely. Andy's father was ordered not to smoke indoors, so he stood in the garage in winter or smoked on the patio in warmer weather. Despite his own smoking, he, too, cautioned Andy not to let tobacco enter his life.

And of course, Andy had heard a few weak messages at school and church about the dangers of smoking. (He'd hear many more if he were growing up today.) He told himself many times that he was not going to become like his father and stand out in a cold garage in order to have a cigarette. My, how that garage stank, especially in winter!

Many temptations

Ironically, it was in that very garage that Andy had his first cigarette. His father had left a pack of cigarettes lying half-camouflaged under his work gloves. There they were, so easy to reach. Andy had just come home from a rough day at school, where his teacher had chided him for not working up to his potential. In the past, he'd seen his father – and his brother, too – turn to cigarettes when they were upset or under stress. And a few days earlier, Andy had seen several of his friends smoking on their way home from school. They'd offered him a puff or two, which he had declined.

Although Andy was not consciously aware of the forces that helped propel that first cigarette into his mouth, it's likely that several influences were at work. His father's smoking was a big factor; parental smoking has always been identified as having a major impact on young beginning smokers. His brother's smoking had perhaps an even greater effect; studies have shown that older siblings can have even more influence than parents on beginner smokers.

Low self-esteem may also have played a role, according to many psychological studies. Andy always felt inadequate next to his older brother, who achieved success with little apparent effort and tended to be a "star" in everything he undertook. In fact, Andy took his first puffs on a cigarette the day a teacher suggested he wasn't working as hard as he might and even implied an unfavorable comparison with his older brother.

Peer-group pressure, a powerful effect on many who begin smoking, was apparently at play as well. Several of Andy's closest friends had been smoking for several months and were urging him to give tobacco a try.

There was the issue of availability. If he hadn't seen his father's cigarettes under those work gloves in the garage, his urge to smoke, at least at that moment, might not have emerged. Not surprisingly, kids are more likely to start smoking when they have easy access to cigarettes.

Another major force was advertising and marketing. The cigarette pack had the same logo and package design that Andy had seen hundreds of times before on billboards, in magazine and newspaper advertisements, and in movies. It was as recognizable to him as a Coca-Cola logo.

Andy's first cigarette was the product of an interplay of forces at work for many years. While it's impossible to specify precisely which influence was the strongest, the combination of parental smoking, sibling smoking, peer-group pressure, poor self-esteem, rebelliousness, depression, anxiety, poor academic performance, and the thrill of trying something new were all important factors in Andy's decision to start smoking.

Selling smoke

Through clever advertising and sophisticated marketing, the tobacco industry has normalized its deadly products and even made them seem desirable, despite all the health-related information young people may be exposed to regarding the dangers of tobacco products.

Tobacco advertising and marketing are strong and pervasive influences. The tobacco industry spends billions of dollars each year in the effort to make its products appear glamorous, sexy, and powerful. Among American industries, the tobacco industry conducts some of the most intense marketing campaigns for its products. Only the automobile industry markets its products more heavily.

The illness and death that smoking produces are mentioned only in the warning labels required by the government. The tobacco industry hides behind these labels when its members are sued for the damage its products inflict on the public, pointing out that statements appear right on cigarette packs warning that use of these products can result in illness and death!

Brands that are most heavily advertised are those that youngsters are most likely to smoke. The effect of tobacco advertising on young people is perhaps best epitomized by R.J. Reynolds Company's introduction of the Joe Camel campaign. After introducing the camel cartoon character in 1988, Camel's share of the adolescent cigarette market increased dramatically – from less than 1 percent before 1988 to 8 percent in 1989 to more than 13 percent in 1993! Fortunately, comic-book-style characters are no longer permitted in tobacco advertisements.

The issue of availability is also important. When cigarettes aren't available to young people, they're less likely to start smoking. Sadly, parents and older siblings leave their tobacco products lying around where curious youngsters can find them. Worse yet is the fact that underage youth can buy tobacco products from some merchants who are only interested in making a few more dollars off kids – despite laws in all 50 states that prohibit cigarette sales to minors.

Numerous merchants sell unpackaged single cigarettes ("loosies") for a few cents, thereby making cigarettes more economically available to young people than a full package that sells for $5 or more. Often, "loosies" are stored low on the counter, where it's easier for youngsters to either purchase or pilfer them. These individual cigarettes are easily stolen and provide young people with ready access to their first cigarettes.

Although the tobacco industry denies it, its own documents reveal that for many decades, it has had an incredibly well-financed strategy of marketing cigarettes to underage youth. Why? Because the tobacco industry loses so many smokers each year to death and quitting, it turns to young people to help replenish its customer base. People are, after all, much less likely to begin smoking once they become adults.

The science of smoking

What happens when a young person takes his or her first few puffs? Almost without exception, those first inhalations are difficult to endure. The human body is simply not equipped to handle the irritating smoke with the multiple poisons it contains – at least initially. Coughing, choking, headache, even feelings of nausea are common reactions.

Some people are lucky. Their body's unpleasant reactions are so harsh that they no longer feel like smoking. These people may not even finish their first cigarette. But unfortunately for others, their bodies adapt, and after the first few puffs, their bodies begin to accept the smoke. And the negative reaction continues to diminish with the next cigarette and then the next. And then something else starts to kick in: the powerful, addicting effects of nicotine.

Nicotine is a "psychoactive" drug. In other words, it produces mood changes. The "buzz" that occurs within seconds of inhaling tobacco smoke is pleasurable to most people. Many have described this feeling as a mixture of relaxation and euphoria, and it's widely believed that nicotine has a direct impact on the pleasure centers of the brain. It's also possible for nicotine to affect emotional states by reducing feelings of fear, anxiety, boredom, and anger while creating a sense of excitement. Smoking thus becomes a means that people use to handle their emotions. Keep this in mind when we describe in detail later in this book why quitting smoking can be quite challenging.

Inhaling cigarette smoke is an extremely rapid and efficient means of delivering nicotine to the brain. Within seven seconds of your first puff, a quarter of the nicotine you inhale passes directly into your brain. Nicotine's rapid effects on your brain produce a strong, pleasurable, and nearly immediate reinforcement of smoking behavior. Or, put simply, when you feel good, you want to continue to feel good again and again and again.

Evidence has recently emerged indicating that cigarette companies have boosted nicotine levels in the cigarette brands that are the most popular among young people. The Massachusetts Department of Public Health released a study in 2006 that examined nicotine levels in more than 100 cigarette brands over a six-year period. The study showed a steady climb in the amount of nicotine added to cigarettes (and then delivered to the lungs of smokers), with overall nicotine yields increasing by about 10 percent. The study also found the three cigarette brands most popular with young people – Marlboro, Newport, and Camel – delivered significantly more nicotine than they had six years earlier. In other words, higher nicotine levels translate into even more rapid addiction – and greater difficulty for the person trying to quit smoking. Thus, addiction to nicotine probably occurs more quickly now than ever.

And who's getting addicted quickly these days?

Each day, more than 6,000 persons under the age of 18 try their first cigarette, and more than 3,000 persons under 18 get hooked and become daily smokers. Eighty percent of these smokers begin smoking before their 18th birthday, despite the fact that this constitutes illegal behavior in all fifty states. Ninety percent begin before the age of 19.

Youth smoking reached its peak in the 1970s when over 35 percent of high school seniors smoked on a regular basis. With the introduction of a variety of school- and community-based prevention programs, the percentage of high school seniors who smoked later dropped to about 30 percent. For reasons not entirely clear – but which many attribute to clever and pervasive marketing by the tobacco companies – it climbed back to its previous levels in the early 1990s. Since the mid-'90s, however, the rate has dropped again.

Now, in 2007, slightly more than one-quarter of high school seniors smoke, with a higher percentage of girls smoking than boys and a higher percentage of whites smoking than Hispanics or African Americans. Factors believed to be behind this drop include school-based programs of education and prevention, restrictions on tobacco advertising, mass-media campaigns, more vigorous attempts to limit youth access to tobacco products, and higher tobacco excise taxes. Research studies have demonstrated that a 10 percent increase in the price of cigarettes reduces overall tobacco consumption by 3 to 5 percent and reduces youth smoking by about 7 percent.

Campaigns for clean indoor air also play a positive role here. These campaigns seek to eliminate exposure to dangerous secondhand smoke in public places. When facilities such as restaurants and shopping malls go smoke-free, smoking becomes less apparent – and appears less normal – to children and adolescents. For many years, smoking has been seen as a normal part of our culture. That smokers must now go outside to smoke is a definite message to youth that there is something inherently wrong with smoking. This is a vital message to convey. Young people can also observe the addictive power of smoking when they see otherwise respectable adults standing outside in all sorts of weather, getting their nicotine "fix."

Easy to start; hard to stop

Andy's progression to regular smoking is similar to the path taken by the more than 1 million youngsters in the United States who take up smoking each year. Andy didn't immediately start to smoke every day. But once his body overcame its initial negative reaction to his first cigarettes, he began smoking more frequently – up to several times a week – and looked forward to his next cigarette and the camaraderie that came with hanging around with his "smoking buddies," a group that was growing larger all the time.

Smoking made him feel "grown-up." It was also a bit of a rebellious act, since both his parents – as well as his schoolteachers – were against his smoking. He paid more attention to where his father hid his cigarettes, and he also "borrowed" cigarettes from his smoking friends. By the time he was 13 years old, he had established several sources of supply, including an older friend who was able to make regular cigarette purchases at a gas station. By the time he was 14, he was smoking several times each day and almost always had his own supply of cigarettes.

At this point, Andy was addicted. His parents found out about his daily smoking and were not pleased. His mother wasn't angry just at Andy; she criticized his father and his older brother Charlie for "setting a bad example." They, of course, argued that they had warned Andy about smoking and urged him not to start. Andy claimed that smoking was "no big deal." Nearly all his friends smoked, and he was sure he could quit if he really wanted to. But in college, when he made his first real (and unsuccessful) attempt at quitting, he was shocked to realize how deeply entrenched smoking was in his life and how addicted he had become. Throughout his adult life, he made many attempts at quitting, only to relapse after periods of abstinence ranging from a few days to more than a year.

Andy did not finally rid himself of tobacco until after he suffered a heart attack at the age of 49. "I knew if I didn't quit then, I might not have any more opportunities," he recently told me. He has remained smoke-free for more than a dozen years, exercises regularly, and reports that he feels healthier than he can remember ever feeling.

Sadly, though, his older brother, Charlie, who never quit, died of lung cancer in his early 60s.

Starting smoking is a journey that begins, unfortunately, all too easily. And once you start on that road, it's pretty much all downhill. Beyond the need to continue buying cigarettes, very little effort is required to keep the addiction going. This stands in stark contrast to the path of quitting, which calls for considerable effort and persistence. Andy would tell you that. He would also tell you how sad – and angry – he is that tobacco dramatically shortened the life of his brother, Charlie. But most of all, he wishes that no one in his family had ever started smoking in the first place.

Chapter 4

How Did the Nicotine Monkey on My Back Grow So Strong?

Joe began smoking at the age of 12 and began drinking about a year later. Both his parents drank and smoked heavily. His school performance was mediocre at best. By the time Joe reached his 21st birthday, his drinking had caused him to lose several jobs as well as his driver's license. He also used drugs (cocaine was his drug of choice) and smoked nearly two packs a day. Because of Joe's abusive lifestyle, his future seemed bleak.

At age 30, he hit rock bottom. He'd been jailed several times, his wife left him, he was unemployed – again – and his health was failing. For the fourth time in his young life, he entered an alcohol and drug rehabilitation program.

When he left rehab, he was clean, and he has remained clean for more than ten years. He reunited with his wife, became a successful salesman, and hasn't touched a drop of alcohol or used any other drug since then. As for his smoking ...

Joe has tried to quit smoking many times. He jokes that he's tried "every smoking-cessation product known to man, and nothing's worked!" Despite his best efforts, he was never able to stop for more than a day or two. "I just don't understand it," he says. "I was able to get off and stay off alcohol and all those other drugs, so why can't I quit smoking?"

Joe is not alone: Many alcoholics and those addicted to other drugs report similar experiences. Smoking was a "gateway drug" for them as it was for Joe, leading to the use of various illegal drugs. People are surprised and amazed to find that quitting smoking and staying smoke-free often turn out to be more challenging than getting off alcohol or hard drugs such as cocaine or heroin. As Joe says, "The actual physical withdrawal of quitting smoking was minor compared to getting off heroin or alcohol, but I had a lot of cravings for a cigarette days and weeks after I'd quit, and I always gave in!"

How does tobacco get such a deep hold on people? What makes tobacco so hard to walk away from? Let's try to answer these questions.

The power of nicotine

For years, tobacco companies and researchers debated whether smoking was "addictive" or "habituating." This was not simply an academic argument over semantics. There are, after all, incredible differences between the grip chocolate and peanuts (which are habituating) have on people, and the grasp heroin and cocaine (which are addictive) have.

Over the years, the tobacco industry collected considerable research of its own that demonstrated how addictive tobacco really is, but it kept this information secret. In its public statements, it denied that its products were addictive. But this denial ended after congressional hearings in 1994, when the chief executive officers of seven major American tobacco companies testified under oath that nicotine was not addictive. Faced with an outcry from scientists and the public as well as possible charges of lying under oath, the tobacco companies backpedaled on this issue. For example, in February 2007, the Philip Morris website (www.philipmorrisusa.com) had this to say about the addictive nature of smoking:

"Philip Morris USA agrees with the overwhelming medical and scientific consensus that cigarette smoking is addictive. It can be very difficult to quit smoking, but this should not deter smokers who want to quit from trying to do so."

Actually, the issue of whether tobacco is addictive was clearly settled for the scientific community and the general public with the landmark 1988 "Report of the Surgeon General." After an exhaustive review of the facts, this report came up with three broad and powerful conclusions:

1. Cigarettes and other forms of tobacco are addicting.

2. Nicotine is the drug in tobacco that causes addiction.

3. The pharmacological and behavioral processes that determine tobacco addiction are similar to those that determine addiction to drugs such as heroin and cocaine.

Within the scientific community, there are three commonly accepted primary criteria for addiction:

- Highly controlled or compulsive use
- Psychoactive effects
- Drug-reinforced behavior

Tobacco clearly meets all three criteria. Regular, addictive smokers – who compose about 95 percent of all smokers – smoke many times each day in highly predictable and repetitive fashion. For example, a smoker will never "forget" to have a cigarette with his or her coffee or "forget" to have a cigarette after a meal. In fact, smoking becomes an extremely repetitive, compulsive behavior even among folks who are not compulsive in other aspects of their lives.

As mentioned earlier, nicotine is a psychoactive (mood-altering) drug that has direct and powerful effects on the brain. Inhaled tobacco smoke is an extremely rapid and efficient means of delivering nicotine to the brain. A smoker receives a pleasurable "buzz" a few seconds after inhaling the smoke. A few puffs can produce temporary changes in mood. If a person is experiencing unpleasant feelings like anger, fear, boredom, or excess excitement, nicotine will dampen or soften those feelings.

Finally, smokers will do things most people perceive as unpleasant (such as standing out in the bitter cold to smoke or driving miles in the middle of the night to buy cigarettes) that become reinforced (rewarded) by the effects of the nicotine in the smoke they inhale. Today, no reputable scientist – or smoker trying to quit – can honestly deny the powerfully addictive properties of nicotine.

Joe continued to drink heavily and use hard drugs even as he knew his life was going down the drain; although he wanted to change, he felt powerless to alter his behavior. This illustrates the core of addictive behavior: the inability of individuals to modify their behavior despite strong desires to do so and highly negative consequences if they do not. Many smokers continue to smoke even after they are diagnosed with cancer, heart disease, lung disease, or any of the many life-shortening diseases caused by tobacco. In other words, nicotine, like other addictions, produces highly irrational behavior even in people who by most other standards conduct their lives in a reasonably rational fashion.

The reason for this seems clear: Addictions work at brain levels beneath the thinking or rational portion of the brain. A big challenge of smoking cessation is to use one's higher brain powers in the cerebral cortex to outsmart the lower (or deep) brain's addiction to nicotine. (More about this later.)

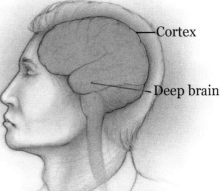

The powerful, addictive properties of nicotine are multiplied by the frequency with which it is used. Smoking is the most overly practiced addiction in the world. Do alcoholics or drug addicts turn to their addictive substances first thing in the morning, after meals, while driving, during a work break, when anxious, while watching television, before retiring to bed – in all, maybe up to forty times or more each day? Not at all. The simple fact is that if you're an average smoker, you smoke much more frequently than an alcoholic drinks or a drug addict takes drugs. Assuming that you take an average of ten puffs per cigarette, if you smoke a pack a day, you'll take in approximately 73,000 nicotine "hits" each year. This means that in less than fifteen years – by the time you're around 30 years old, if you're a typical smoker – you'll have received over a million nicotine hits!

A pack-a-day smoker who smokes for twenty years smokes the equivalent of a single cigarette over nine miles long!

Put another way, if you smoke a pack a day for twenty years, you'll smoke a total of 146,000 cigarettes. Since the average length of a cigarette is about four inches, the total length of all the cigarettes you smoke over twenty years will equal more than 48,600 feet – or more than nine miles!

There are some other important facts about nicotine that you should know. One is that if you're hooked on nicotine, you develop urges for it when your body's typical levels of nicotine start to decline. This urge is strong enough to cause some smokers to beg total strangers for a cigarette when their supply runs out, or to tolerate chest-racking coughs as they light their first cigarette of the day, or as Brian did (*see Chapter 1*), drag themselves out of a hospital bed and down several flights of stairs for a cigarette! Most smokers begin to experience these urges within an hour of their last cigarette, others within twenty minutes. While these urges impel people to smoke, most smokers learn how to cope when they can't satisfy their urges right away – a fact well worth remembering when it comes to quitting altogether.

It should be noted that when smokers go for longer periods without smoking – for example, several hours or more, as they do when they're attempting to quit – most develop some withdrawal symptoms in addition to their craving for nicotine. These withdrawal symptoms include both physical and psychological complaints. We will address how to cope with withdrawal symptoms later in this book.

The power of habit

As early as she could remember, Linda enjoyed movies and popcorn. They just went together. Whenever she went to the movies with her parents, grandparents, or friends, she simply had to have a box of popcorn. As soon as she was on her way to the theater – before she could smell the butter or hear the delightful sound of it popping – she began to think about ordering a brightly colored box of her favorite snack. Even if she'd just finished a large meal and didn't think she could consume another bite, if she was heading to the cinema, she knew there would be room in her stomach for popcorn. For Linda, watching a movie and eating popcorn had become linked together, and this linkage continues today – not just for Linda, but for a surprisingly large segment of the population. Just listen to the chewing going on around you the next time you go to a movie.

Whenever a particular behavior (eating popcorn) occurs in a specific situation (watching a movie), an association between the behavior and the situation is formed. This is one of the most basic – and most powerful – types of learning. The more this association is repeated, the stronger it becomes. For Linda, just being in the theater was enough to set off a strong desire for popcorn.

People often refer to smoking as "a bad habit." While it's certainly bad for our health and longevity, it's more than a single habit. Smoking is in fact *many* habits. Because people typically smoke in different situations, smoking behavior becomes associated with these many situations. The more the associations (sometimes called cues, linkages, or triggers) are repeated, the stronger they become. People smoke when they rise in the morning, while having their cup of coffee, while driving to work, during coffee breaks, after lunch, while driving home, while relaxing at home, after dinner, while watching television, before retiring to bed, and so forth. The specific pattern, of course, varies from smoker to smoker; for example, some people have strong linkages between smoking and work, while others – who are not permitted to smoke at work – do not.

Just as the sight of a movie theater was all it took to stimulate Linda's desire for popcorn, so the presence of one of these linkages is enough to kindle a desire to smoke. And just as Linda craved popcorn even when she wasn't hungry, so will a smoking linkage prompt a desire to smoke even when the smoker has no great need to feed a nicotine depletion. This fact becomes especially important during quitting, since smoking linkages will bring forth desires to smoke long after an individual is no longer actively addicted to nicotine.

For most smokers, smoking becomes linked to a vast assortment of situations in a smoker's life. But smoking doesn't become associated only with outward circumstances – it also becomes associated with emotional states. Smokers smoke when they feel anxious, angry, frustrated, bored, depressed, or worried – indeed, when they're feeling almost any unpleasant emotion. Yet they also smoke when they're happy, relieved, excited, joyful, upbeat, or experiencing other pleasant emotions.

We know that nicotine is a psychoactive drug that tends to "muffle" or soften strong emotions. So, while smoking is linked to emotions of all types, the nicotine in tobacco seems to modify the experience of the emotion itself. It seems to become a crutch for the smoker, helping him cope with strong emotions.

Associations also develop between smoking and people in a smoker's life. Another term for these associations is "smoking buddies." Virtually every smoker has them. They smoke together, and in fact their relationship is built around smoking. The appearance of a smoking buddy will often bring out a desire to smoke just as surely as a cup of coffee or a strong feeling of frustration will. It's especially important to know how to deal with these smoking buddies when it comes time for quitting, since not only will their presence set off a desire to smoke, but these folks are potentially a source of resupply (and relapse) to the would-be quitter.

Psychological meanings of smoking

Ralph began smoking when he was about 14. As with many young people his age, he began smoking with his peer group, to be one of the guys. But soon his smoking seemed to take on a new meaning for him: protection from his father!

Ralph grew up in a very achievement-oriented family. No matter how hard he worked or how well he performed, it never seemed to be enough to really satisfy his parents – especially his father, he says. "I discovered that smoking somehow helped protect me from my very critical and demanding father."

Ralph describes his situation as though he were "hiding behind my smoke," so that when his father criticized him and urged him to work even harder, his smoking seemed to shield him emotionally from the full impact of his father's demands. We know from the way nicotine works that his smoking probably softened his strong emotional reaction to his father's criticism.

Now, at 42, Ralph wanted to quit smoking. After all, he was a physician who knew all too well how smoking ravages health and shortens lives. He urged his patients to quit, and he took great satisfaction when they were able to take his advice and successfully stop smoking. Still, he continued to smoke regularly, becoming what is often described as a "closet smoker" – someone who smokes alone, secretively, and, in Ralph's case, with considerable guilt and self-loathing. When asked, "Why do you smoke?" Ralph replied, "Because, as crazy as it sounds, I feel as though it somehow protects me now, just as it seemed to protect me years ago from my father."

Ralph knew that smoking shielded him from nothing and, in fact, actually increased his vulnerability to many diseases. Yet here he was, believing, on an emotional level, that his smoking somehow protected him! Though the idea was totally irrational – and he knew it was – it also seemed entirely real. Ralph was giving smoking what psychologists call a "false attribution."

To Ralph, the psychological meaning of his smoking was that it somehow shielded him from negative scrutiny and possible criticism from others.

Do other smokers make such false attributions, giving smoking credit for playing important roles in their lives? In order to attempt to answer this question, 200 smokers who were seeking help to quit were asked, "Why do you smoke? And what does smoking do for you?" Every smoker gave at least one answer. Not surprisingly, many gave more than one reason.

Table 1
Some Common Psychological Meanings of Smoking

1. Smoking is an "old friend" or companion who is always there.
2. It's a special means of handling stress, especially severe stress.
3. It's a means of muffling anger (and other unpleasant emotions).
4. It's a way of "buying time."
5. It expands one's abilities (e.g., writing, problem-solving, handling difficult or ambiguous situations).
6. It's an irreplaceable source of pleasure in one's life.
7. It's a means of rewarding oneself after an accomplishment.

Table 1 presents the seven most common psychological reasons that people smoke, the most common being that cigarettes are "an old friend." Smokers who have gone through rough times in their lives point to their cigarettes as companions that have stayed by their side, no matter what. "To me, quitting smoking is like losing my best friend" is a frequently heard statement in smoking-cessation groups. Also heard is the comment that smoking is a means of handling stress – especially intense or prolonged stress. Some say that it allows them to tolerate upset and continue functioning, perhaps by "muffling" (buffering) anger and other emotions, a property of nicotine described earlier.

Some see smoking as a means of "buying time," especially in situations requiring complicated decisions. "When facing a difficult situation that I'm not sure how to deal with, I have a cigarette, take a little 'time-out,' and think about it," some say. Others perceive smoking as enhancing their abilities; for example, there are smokers who believe they work better at their computer if they have a cigarette in their hand. Others say, "There's no way I could do my taxes if I weren't smoking!"

Some smokers describe smoking as an irreplaceable source of pleasure in their lives and feel that quitting will create a drab, joyless existence. Others use smoking as a means of rewarding themselves after an accomplishment, like the student who smokes after finishing a difficult chapter in a textbook or a set of math problems, or a gardener who lights up after finishing a series of chores.

Smoking has other psychological meanings in addition to those mentioned in Table 1. While they may have little if any factual basis, they seem very real to the smoker and appear to have a powerful impact, especially when the smoker thinks about quitting. Later in this book we'll explore these psychological meanings, paying particular attention to the ways in which they are essentially false assumptions.

To summarize, three main factors appear to sustain the powerful behavior of smoking. Smoking becomes deeply embedded in a person's life through:

- The powerfully addicting properties of nicotine
- The many associations that come to exist between smoking and situations, emotions, and persons in the smoker's life
- The special attributions (psychological meanings) that smokers give to smoking

It's no wonder that permanently stopping smoking becomes a real challenge to the would-be quitter. Yet despite the complex and challenging nature of the task, many millions of people from all walks of life have successfully overcome their cigarette addictions – including Joe, whom we met earlier in this chapter.

How do they do it? Let's look at the quitting process.

Chapter 5

Planning to Get That Nicotine Monkey off My Back

Sound preparation is essential to a successful journey, yet no matter how thoroughly you map out a trip, surprises occasionally occur. In this chapter, we'll look at the process of quitting smoking the same way we'd plan for a journey, and we'll recommend steps you can take to circumvent surprises and maximize the chances of reaching the destination of a tobacco-free life.

An overview of quitting

How do people quit smoking? In theory, the answer is simple and can be described in a few paragraphs. In practice, the process is a bit more complex.

In theory, you decide to quit. You may pick a quitting day or throw away the pack of cigarettes on impulse. Still, you've made a decision.

Within a few hours after your last cigarette, if you're like most quitting smokers you'll experience one or more withdrawal symptoms. These symptoms usually peak in severity in one to three days, then gradually weaken over the next ten days or so, and are pretty much a thing of the past after two weeks, as nicotine is eliminated from your body. As we'll discuss later, this course of withdrawal symptoms may be substantially changed if you're using some type of medication, such as nicotine replacement.

Even after your body is free of nicotine, however, cravings continue. As described in Chapter 4, cravings or urges for a cigarette are not simply the result of diminished nicotine levels in the body. Because of the many, many linkages or triggers you've developed – associations between situations and smoking, emotions and smoking, and people and smoking – each time you're in the presence of one or more of these linkages, you'll experience a craving.

But each time you *don't* smoke in the presence of these linkages, one or more of these associations will be weakened. Psychologists call this a process of *extinction*, or breaking the connection between stimulus and response that sustains a behavior. For example, you have a cup of coffee without having a cigarette, you drive to work without having a cigarette, and you feel bored but you don't light a cigarette. The bonds between coffee and smoking, driving and smoking, and boredom and smoking gradually weaken.

Eventually, these associations diminish to the point where your experience of having a cup of coffee, driving to work, or feeling boredom no longer has the power to arouse your urge to smoke. Many former smokers describe being amazed when they finally get to the point that they never even think of having a cigarette with coffee or after a meal, or while driving. A common response is: "I never thought I'd ever get to this point – it's amazing!"

Over time, as you deal with a variety of situations and stressors without smoking, you gradually realize that your personal "psychological meanings" of smoking were in fact myths. For example, you develop a clearer perspective about how much of a "friend" smoking really is once it's gone and you realize that you're feeling healthier, less stressed, and more vigorous. Or you realize that you're quite capable of handling difficult tasks without smoking – and you even feel stronger for not relying on the nicotine crutch.

How quitting happens in real life

Joe, the recovering alcoholic and drug user we met in Chapter 4, did not consider smoking a major issue when he went through rehab. After all, it was his drinking and drug use that had wrought havoc in his life, not his smoking. Or so he thought – until his physician saw changes in the tissues of his mouth that suggested a high potential for the development of oral cancer, a disease frequently caused by smoking, often in combination with heavy drinking. That news hit Joe like a ton of bricks: "After all these years of alcoholism and drug addiction, wouldn't it be ironic if cigarettes kill me at an early age?"

Until he received that high-impact news from his physician, Joe had never really given a serious thought to quitting smoking. He was in what psychologist Dr. James Prochaska and his colleagues describe, in their brilliant work on how people change, as the *precontemplation stage*. People in this state of mind don't even consider the possibility of quitting. While they may have some awareness of the potential benefits of being smoke-free, in their minds they also anticipate the costs – the potential difficulty involved in the quitting process, along with the loss in their lives of nicotine and its pleasurable effects. To them, the costs outweigh the benefits.

The news from his doctor hit Joe hard. He began to look at his cigarettes differently; in fact, he reported that after this news, his cigarettes did not seem to taste as good as they once did. He talked with his wife, who had never pressured him to quit, although she had let him know that she'd certainly welcome and support his quitting once he made the decision. She urged him to try.

For the first time since he started smoking at age 12, Joe began thinking seriously about quitting smoking. He was entering Prochaska's second stage of change, the *contemplation stage*, defined as the intention to change (quit smoking) sometime within the next six months.

About two months later, Joe asked his physician to help him quit and took his doctor's advice about enrolling in a smoking-cessation program. Joe was now in the *preparation stage* – he was planning to take action in the immediate future. Two weeks after enrolling in that program, he decided to quit smoking. He was now in the *action stage*, meaning that he was actually giving up cigarettes and beginning a new, tobacco-free life.

Despite Joe's good intentions, his quitting did not last long. A few days later, Joe found himself in what seemed to be an interminable traffic jam. He saw a man in the car in front of him smoking heavily throughout the traffic tie-up. My, that looked good to him! When he finally escaped from the crawling traffic and was refueling his automobile, the urge to buy a pack of cigarettes was irresistible. He gave in, promising himself that he'd have "only a couple." Two days later, he was smoking at the same level as he had before he quit. Joe had experienced what all too often becomes a stage for many who quit smoking – *relapse*. He also began to learn something extremely important: When people quit smoking, they cannot have a cigarette now and then. If they do, it virtually guarantees relapse.

After several tries and several subsequent relapses, Joe finally managed to escape the clutches of his cigarettes for good. He entered what Prochaska terms the *maintenance stage*. This is the point at which people work to prevent relapse and maintain their change. Maintenance, as defined by Prochaska, lasts between about six months and five years.

Finally, the *termination stage* of smoking is characterized by total confidence and zero temptation. This stage may not be fully reached for years. Joe has now reached it, nearly six years after he quit for good.

Surveys of smokers demonstrate that most of them know that smoking is hazardous; most smokers would like to quit sometime. However, at any given time, about four in ten smokers are in the *precontemplation stage* and not even thinking about quitting; another four in ten are in the *contemplation stage* and thinking about quitting; and less than two in ten are actually in the *preparation* and *action* stages, getting ready for and/or actually working toward cessation.

Mental preparation

Some smokers seem to quit on impulse, while others plan ahead quite thoroughly. Which is best?

Anecdotes abound about smokers who impulsively threw away their cigarettes and never smoked again. There are also tales of smokers who threw away their packs, only to retrieve them from the garbage can a few hours later!

Many of those who appear to quit on impulse actually may have been planning this action for a long time. Most research suggests that some form of preparation is more likely to lead to success. Any form of preparation – even if it's just getting rid of all the smoking materials in the house – can help you arrange your situation to maximize your chances for success.

Done correctly, proper mental preparation can be a vitally important aspect of quitting. As we mentioned earlier, quitting smoking is a journey – one of the most important and beneficial journeys you can take. Think of it this way: Imagine that you're planning a trip across the country to attend your best friend's wedding. Along the way, rough weather hits and one of your connecting flights is delayed for several hours. What an inconvenience! Perhaps you have to stay overnight in the airport. But if you're really committed to the journey, you'll do whatever is required to keep going until you get to the wedding. No matter what it takes, you'll be there.

That frame of mind should be present when you quit smoking. All too often, smokers are more *technique-oriented* than *journey-oriented*. They focus more on the smoking-cessation techniques that might be available – from the nicotine patch to hypnosis to counseling – than they do on committing themselves unequivocally to the process or journey of quitting. Although many of these techniques can be helpful, nothing can substitute for the proper mental preparation. Imagine a traveler concentrating more on types of aircraft and seats available on a particular route than on committing to the trip itself!

Smokers who are committed to the process or journey of quitting will typically respond with a simple "Yes" when asked whether they really mean to quit. Smokers less dedicated will often give lengthier replies such as "I've tried so many different things – I hope something works for me this time." This type of response seems to suggest that the smoker is looking for something that will effortlessly remove the addiction. The basic truth is that there is *no* magic bullet to make smoking just go away, or to stop cravings with little or no discomfort. Just as a long physical journey can (and usually does) produce some frustration or hardship, so does the journey of quitting smoking sometimes evoke negative feelings.

Very often the results of *not* quitting are many, many times more uncomfortable than any discomfort associated with quitting: painful medical procedures, major operations, debilitating diseases, and shortened lives. For many smokers, the most uncomfortable and ultimately tragic consequence of continuing to smoke is the remorse that comes of knowing that the deadly downside of smoking could have been prevented if only they had acted earlier and quit. If only they had done what many millions have done to preserve their health and committed themselves once and for all to becoming nonsmokers, *doing whatever it took to reach that goal*. A deep commitment to the process of quitting is the single most important characteristic of smokers who successfully quit.

In the 1970s, a major producer of automotive oil filters used this catchy slogan: "Pay me now or pay me later." The advertisement featured a garage mechanic who asserted that automobile owners had a choice: They could choose to pay a few dollars there and then for a new oil filter – or several hundred dollars later for major engine repairs. This slogan can be used to describe some of the mental process underlying successful preparation for quitting. Commit yourself wholeheartedly to a process that involves work, persistence, and some discomfort. In return for completing the journey, you are likely to avoid the debilitating diseases and distress produced by smoking. And in the process of successfully quitting, you get another, less anticipated benefit: You are proud of your accomplishment and feel much better about yourself as a result. What journey can provide more positive outcomes than that?

This is the type of thinking that you should plant deeply in your mind as you make your plans to quit.

Picking a quit date

Unless you quit on impulse (this does work for some), you need to select a "quit date." This date should not be set too far in the future. When Joan tried to quit, she selected New Year's Day, which is a very popular quitting date. The only problem was that she chose this date the previous Fourth of July!

Selecting a date too far in the future can result in your motivation to quit waning during the intervening time. By the time New Year's Day rolled around, Joan's commitment was sagging and she found plenty of excuses to postpone her quit date further – for example, a snowstorm was coming. (And heavy snowfalls are always stressful!) Postponing the quit date can be a real problem – a "reason" can always be found for postponing the date even further.

When Joan finally succeeded in becoming tobacco-free, she selected a quit date about a three weeks away. For most people, a quit date somewhere between a week and a month away is optimal.

You shouldn't pick a vacation day or quit just before a vacation begins. People typically associate vacations with going easy on themselves. This is not a good frame of mind to be in when you're beginning the actual journey of quitting!

Quitting smoking is a journey that requires some effort and self-discipline. For most people, making the quit date a regular, routine day works best. It's better to quit during the workweek than over the weekend, since for most smokers, there are many more opportunities to smoke away from work. Also, picking a day when no unusual stresses are anticipated makes excellent sense. But once you choose that quit day, you shouldn't modify it just because things are becoming more stressful than you anticipated. Barring an unforeseen major event or catastrophe, you should begin the journey as originally planned.

As Joan's case illustrates, most smokers can be remarkably creative in coming up with reasons why their chosen quit date isn't so good after all. Just as you wouldn't postpone an important trip because it's raining or snowing, don't postpone one of the most significant journeys of your life because some unanticipated event or stress appears.

Should you announce your quit date to friends, family, and co-workers? Telling people is certainly a way of strengthening your commitment to quit, so it's likely to be helpful. But some smokers don't wish to tell, perhaps for fear of public embarrassment if they don't succeed or because they're concerned about how others will react to them once they actually quit. So, there's no hard and fast rule here. Announcing your plans to embark on an important journey is less important than making a strong personal commitment to that journey.

Weakening the strongest linkages

After picking your quit date, you should make a careful – and honest – appraisal of your *strongest* linkages. In other words, which cigarettes are most deeply embedded – and prized – in your daily routine?

Perhaps the first cigarette in the morning is the one you cherish. Maybe you have a very strong linkage with coffee or with driving. You should choose your *three strongest linkages* and work on weakening them before you actually quit altogether. If a targeted linkage is the first cigarette of the morning, then you should delay that cigarette by at least twenty minutes. If it's coffee, then you should stop smoking while you're drinking coffee and not light up until the coffee is finished. If it's driving, then you should lock your cigarettes in the trunk before you get behind the wheel. In other words, while you're moving toward your quit date, you're weakening three of your strongest linkages.

This way, by the time you quit smoking completely, you'll have mastered some of the toughest smoking situations. And the knowledge that you've confronted and broken some of your strongest linkages will give rise to a sense of inner strength.

Reducing consumption

One of the times Joe tried to quit, he reduced his smoking to one cigarette each day. My, how he looked forward to that cigarette – he would count the hours! He'd wait until he arrived home after work, go into the basement, and retrieve a cigarette from his special hiding place. Because his body had had nearly twenty-four hours since his last cigarette to clear the nicotine (and other poisons) from his body, this cigarette really hit him hard – reminding him, in fact, of the powerful "hit" he used to feel when he used cocaine years before. That cigarette became a highlight of his day.

Reducing consumption to one or two cigarettes a day before quitting is not a recommended practice, since it tends to increase the powerful "buzz" when smoking does occur, thereby rewarding the act of smoking even more than usual.

But reducing smoking to some degree before quitting can be an important part of preparation. If you consistently refrain from smoking in the presence of the three strongest linkages (as described above), this in itself will reduce consumption.

A good general rule is to get down to one pack (or less) per day before you actually quit. This is especially important if you're a really heavy smoker and smoke two packs or more each day. If you're down to a pack when quitting day arrives, you can expect less withdrawal and a generally easier time of quitting than if you're smoking two or three packs a day.

Changing smoking patterns

People don't just smoke; they smoke Camels. Or Marlboros. Or Virginia Slims. In other words, you're highly disposed to smoke your own brand and will smoke another brand only if yours is not available.

Just before Joe quit successfully, he switched from his brand to another that he really didn't like. Not only did this reduce the reward value of each cigarette; it was a constant reminder that he'd be quitting soon, thus contributing to his mental preparation for quitting. Clearly, changing brands can assist in the preparation phase.

Throwing away your lighter and using matches instead is another change that can benefit your overall quitting process. There's a ritual to smoking that often includes the feel and sound of a lighter as it sparks the flame that ignites the cigarette. After many thousands of repetitions, your use of a lighter becomes highly automatic. Giving away – or, preferably, throwing away – your lighter represents another aspect of genuine commitment to quitting. Each time you use a match to light a cigarette, it's a reminder of the quitting process. And when you taste the sulfur of the match, it can be a reminder to you that there are more than 4,000 chemicals in cigarette smoke that don't taste as bad as sulfur, but are much more dangerous than that annoying sulfur taste.

Carrying cigarettes in a different place can also be an important part of your preparation for quitting. After you've reached for a cigarette in the same few places thousands and thousands of times, this action becomes quite automatic. Men who typically carry their cigarettes in a front pocket should carry them somewhere else, perhaps in a trouser pocket. Women who have kept their cigarettes in their purses for years should put them in a different place, such as a coat pocket. At home, you should move your cigarettes from their usual place to a new, less convenient location.

These and the other changes described above are designed to shake up your smoking process by making it a less automatic and more conscious course of action. It reminds you that your days of smoking are numbered, so that when quitting day rolls around, some of the automatic behaviors you associate with smoking will be a little weaker, which should strengthen the overall quitting process.

Keeping a smoking diary for several days (or even a week or two) before you quit can be very useful to your preparation process. A smoking diary is simply a small notebook or sheet of paper that tracks your smoking behavior. For each cigarette smoked, you record:

- The number of the cigarette (first of the day, second of the day, etc.)
- The time of day you smoked the cigarette
- A one- or two-word description of the circumstances in which you smoked the cigarette
- Who (if anybody) was with you at the time
- A one- or two-word description of your prevailing mood at the time

Smoking Diary

# of cigarettes	Time of day	Situation	People	Mood
1	7:45 a.m.	After breakfast	Family	Rushed
2	8:20 a.m.	At work	Alone	Normal
3	9:35 a.m.	Coffee break	Co-workers	Pleasant
4	11:45 a.m.	Outside office	With boss	Overwhelmed
5	3:45 p.m.	Coffee break	Co-worker (Ed)	Bored
6	5:45 p.m.	Driving home	Alone	Frustrated
7	7:20 p.m.	Watching TV	Wife	Relaxed

Figure 2: A sample smoking diary kept by an office worker.

In addition to making the smoking process more conscious and less automatic for you, keeping this type of diary gives you a clearer indication of the relative strengths of the various linkages in your smoking life. There is also evidence that simply recording a behavior can alter its frequency; for example, among dieters, keeping a diary of every bit of food eaten and calories ingested has been shown to reduce eating significantly.

Although keeping a smoking diary does reduce smoking and helps people prepare for quitting, many smokers find this task so burdensome that they have great difficulty completing it. If this happens, it's probably best to put aside the diary and focus on other ways of preparing to quit.

Smokers who are able to keep a smoking diary for several days before actually quitting usually report that they learned something important about their smoking patterns.

Thinking the right thoughts about quitting

Smokers who anticipate quitting often report feeling a sense of dread about the road ahead. Stories abound about the difficulties associated with quitting – the withdrawal symptoms, the cravings, the loss of emotional control. Most of these stories are exaggerations. As with any significant journey, however, there may be some discomfort associated with the experience.

But there are also substantial benefits to be reaped, and these benefits begin almost immediately after you quit. The first and one of the most lasting is the pride you'll feel about yourself for undertaking the journey to become tobacco-free. Most people also begin to feel healthier almost from the first day that they quit – and they *are* healthier, too! For example, your heart function and blood pressure improve within the first twenty-four hours after the last cigarette.

It's critically important for you to maintain a positive attitude about quitting and not talk yourself into defeat before you actually begin the quitting process. After all, nearly 50 million Americans have quit smoking, and probably every one at some point had major doubts about whether he or she would be able to finish this journey. (I know I did!)

One way for you to keep yourself on the right path is to anticipate how you might handle certain situations once you've quit. For example, if you work in an office, how would you handle the overload and pressure that seems to occur at some point nearly every day? You might decide that when the pressure hits, you'll simply take a "clean-air break" instead of your former "cigarette break" and go for a brisk walk. Or if your drive to and from work often involves frustrating traffic jams, you may use deep-breathing relaxation techniques when you're caught in stopped traffic.

In short, while you're preparing to quit, you can review your daily life in the locations where you typically smoke and plan how to cope with these situations when you're no longer smoking. In the process, you need to remind yourself of a basic fact: Every situation in life which seems to evoke

the need to smoke can be handled just as effectively – if not more so – *without* smoking. You also need to remind yourself that there is no gift you can receive that's more precious or longer-lasting than quitting smoking. And you're about to give yourself that priceless gift! What journey could be more exciting?

Chapter 6

Quitting: Goodbye to That Nicotine Monkey

In this chapter, we'll discuss some of the basic principles of quitting. These principles are relevant whether you're quitting on your own or participating in an organized cessation program. In the next few chapters, we'll consider products that can help you quit and ways to maintain a smoke-free life.

Quitting on one's own

Millions of people have quit smoking over the years *without* formal treatment programs or cessation devices. It's pretty likely that these "self-quitters" didn't go it totally alone – they may have sought advice from other quitters, read self-help materials (such as this book), or listened to media discussions of quitting, which helped their efforts along the way. It's also pretty likely that these people had tried quitting several times – some as many as six or eight times – before they actually succeeded in becoming smoke-free.

Whether or not you've made a serious attempt to quit on your own before, you should approach your quit date in a determined and resolute state of mind. You may well succeed! But even if you experience a setback, you'll undoubtedly learn a lot about yourself and your smoking behaviors, and you'll be able to use this new information about yourself when you turn to other smoking-cessation strategies.

Remember: *There's no such thing as failure, unless you give up on trying to quit.*

A guide to quitting on your own, the "DeNelsky-Plesec Stop Smoking Checklist," appears in Appendix 1. This list is arranged in a form similar to what an airplane pilot might refer to before takeoff and landing. It describes actions to take as you prepare for quitting, what to do during the first two weeks of quitting, and how to remain smoke-free after two weeks and after two months.

The role of willpower

People often talk about the importance of willpower in quitting smoking. Without question, commitment to quitting and persistence are important components of success. Behavior-modification specialists explain, however, that willpower – typically defined as "the strength of will to carry out one's decisions, wishes, or plans" – depends greatly upon how you arrange a situation. For example, if you plan to go on a diet and you're highly vulnerable to sweets, stocking your house with ice cream, cake, cookies, and similar items is going to make it mighty difficult for willpower to prevail.

One of the most important components of willpower is an environment that's organized to minimize temptations. It's much easier to resist cookies and ice cream if these treats are miles away on the shelves of a store and not in your kitchen cupboard and freezer.

This principle is vitally important when it comes to quitting smoking. Smoking is to a large degree driven by your lower brain's acquired need for nicotine and your specific experiences with smoking. We must use our higher brain powers – our powers of thinking and planning – to outsmart and out-plan our lower brain's cravings for nicotine.

Picking the precise time for quitting

The big day has arrived! The quit day is a very significant day in your life – a day as momentous as a birthday or anniversary – if quitting leads to a permanently smoke-free life. This is where proper planning really pays off. Success often depends upon the actions you take during the initial stages of the quitting process.

In the last chapter, we recommended that you pick your quit date. Now it's time to get even more precise: You should pick the exact time of day for quitting.

Some people will smoke their last cigarette the night before, some will do it early in their quitting day, and others will wait until later. There is no research that recommends one time over another, but it's important to pick a time that you think will work best for you. After all, you're in control of this process.

But without such a preplanned time, it's quite conceivable that quitting day may come and go while you're still smoking – and smoking the next day as well.

Getting rid of all cigarettes

Getting rid of *all* cigarettes is extremely important. Just as an alcoholic must not leave a convenient bottle of scotch stashed away in the kitchen, you should place as much distance as possible between yourself and any tobacco. Ray's case is a good example of why.

Ray was 36 years old when he quit smoking. He was doing quite well several weeks later, just before his relapse. He had *almost* disposed of all the cigarettes in his life. But he had forgotten one last pack – in the glove compartment of his automobile.

Actually, he hadn't really forgotten it – he knew of its existence – but he felt that it would do no harm there. In fact, he rationalized (as many do) that having a pack available would help him think less about and be less troubled by the absence of cigarettes in his life. (This is another example of the amazing power nicotine addiction has to influence rational thinking.)

A few months later, a freak storm hit Ray's area without warning and transformed the roads into treacherous sheets of ice. Ray was driving on an interstate highway in a rural area when he was stopped, along with many others, by several minor accidents in the road ahead of him. Later, his car slid off the road, too. Thankfully, he wasn't injured and his car wasn't damaged.

Because of the road conditions, he was stuck in an uncomfortable situation for several hours before any type of rescue arrived. What should he do? Because he was quite frustrated and angered by his situation – emotions that in the past had strong linkages with smoking – he felt a strong urge for a cigarette. The urge was altogether predictable; after all, not enough time had elapsed since Ray had quit smoking for him to sever all his major associations between smoking and the events and emotions of his daily life.

Had Ray arranged the situation properly from the outset by removing all immediate sources of tobacco, this crisis and his urge for a cigarette would have come and gone without anything happening. But he remembered that pack of cigarettes in the glove compartment and before he knew it, he had smoked several from this pack. Then, even after his car was towed out of the median and he was on his way again, he continued to smoke. *His crisis was over, but his smoking continued.*

Actually, he smoked for several more years, until major health changes made it imperative that he quit again.

This example illustrates the critical importance of getting rid of *all* the cigarettes in your life. If you're discarding your remaining cigarettes in places to which you'll continue to have access (like your own wastebasket), make those cigarettes completely unusable by soaking them in water first. Also remove ashtrays, matches, and other smoking paraphernalia that remind you of smoking.

If you live with someone who smokes, it's quite appropriate to ask that person not to leave cigarettes or ashtrays lying around. Folks who would never eat left-over food tossed into a garbage can have been known to have a drag from a spouse's cigarette butt left in an ashtray. And one drag may be all that's needed to derail a serious quitting attempt. Respect the addictive power of nicotine, and keep its source as far away as possible.

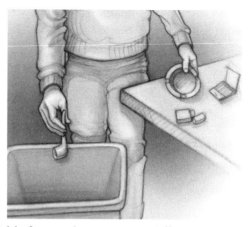

Every ex-smoker is certainly aware that cigarettes are still available for purchase in many different places. But the act of buying cigarettes, or even "bumming" one from a friend, requires more complex action than simply reaching into a dresser drawer or a glove compartment for a hidden pack. Put as much distance as you can between yourself and all cigarettes!

Ray's relapse story illustrates another point. Once you've quit, smoking is no longer an option. *No matter what happens.* There can be *no* exceptions, no matter what kind of crisis occurs. Otherwise, it's just a matter of time until a relapse takes place, since crises happen to everyone, sooner or later.

This is the "Basic Rule" for preventing relapse: *Smoking is no longer an option in my life!*

Spending time with nonsmokers

One critically important part of planning involves the people you'll spend time with right after quitting. Just as recovering alcoholics are advised not to spend time with former drinking buddies, it's imperative for smokers who are quitting to avoid their "smoking buddies," at least for the first few weeks.

Friends and acquaintances who are still smoking represent a double peril: Not only is their very presence a linkage (cue) for smoking, but they also represent a potential source of resupply for you after you've stopped. This means that if you used to take a cigarette break with other smokers, you need to take your breaks somewhere else, even if it means taking your breaks alone. One good alternative (if available) is to take a brisk walk in clean air, away from smokers and smoking.

Managing your social encounters for the first weeks after you quit is also critically important. You need to anticipate and avoid the high-risk situations – places where people may be smoking, such as bars, smoking areas in restaurants, bowling alleys, bingo parlors, and parties where smoking is permitted. Thankfully, due to clean indoor-air movements, fewer and fewer such places exist. And if you're invited to a party in a person's home, use good judgment.

Also avoid places where alcohol is served. For many smokers, very strong linkages exist between smoking and alcohol. In addition, alcohol has the power to turn off the higher powers of the brain, making thinking and planning less reliable. Many new ex-smokers relapse after a drink or two, especially in the presence of smokers who are also drinking.

Instead of picking a high-risk situation like a bar, choose lower-risk situations where smoking is prohibited: libraries, museums, theaters, retail stores, and the like. These locations are not typically associated with smoking, nor are they convenient places for finding tobacco. For example, spending a few hours in a library in the evening may be an excellent alternative to going to a bar or even spending time at home – especially if a good deal of your smoking went on at home. Arranging the situation properly can maximize the likelihood of success.

For many persons, smoking is strongly linked to coffee consumption (or, for some, soft drinks). Does this mean that you should also give up coffee? Not necessarily – trying to give up both nicotine and caffeine at the same time may be unnecessarily challenging! The key here is not to linger for long periods with your coffee cup, thereby prolonging the strong linkage with smoking. Drink the coffee as quickly as possible and then move on. This may require cooling the coffee a bit so that it may be consumed more quickly. Gradually, the linkage between smoking and coffee will weaken and you will be able to return to a more leisurely cup of coffee. This process of minimizing the amount of time spent in the presence of strong linkages may be applied to many other situations in addition to coffee, especially during the early stages of quitting.

One especially critical issue has to do with continuing to live with smokers after you've quit smoking. In all likelihood, strong linkages exist here, since you all probably smoked together. One solution is to ask the people who still smoke not to do so in your presence and also not to leave smoking materials lying around. If these requests are not practical or not heeded, then you should leave the area where others are smoking as quickly as possible.

Again, increasing willpower by reducing temptations is crucial. Put as much distance as you can between yourself and all cigarettes!

Personal behavioral changes that can help

Many experts recommend that new ex-smokers find some type of substitute for smoking, at least in the beginning of the quitting journey. Since there seems to be a tendency for many people to turn to some form of sweets or other high-calorie foods – which can cause weight gain and other problems down the line – choosing a healthy substitute from the beginning makes sense. For many, simply having a bottle of water to sip on, perhaps flavored with a lemon slice, works quite well. Others may choose substitutes like sugarless gum or carrot sticks. Gum can be particularly helpful, since it's not possible for most people to eat while they have chewing gum in their mouths.

In the past, it was customary for quitting smokers to turn to lemon drops, jellybeans, or other candies. The problem here is that adding twenty or more pieces of candy to your diet each day can add significant calories. Some people carry a toothbrush and brush their teeth several times each day, which stimulates their mouths and reminds them of how much fresher their breath is now that they have quit smoking.

In addition to the need for something in their mouths that's not a cigarette, some people report that "their hands have nothing to do" now that they no longer have cigarettes to hold and manipulate. For these people, having something to handle – a pencil, rubber ball, paper clip, or marble – may be useful.

It's important for you to keep active during the first few weeks after quitting. This doesn't mean you should undertake a rigorous exercise program right away; indeed, you should consult your physician before you begin any strenuous new activities. But walking, doing some mild exercises, swimming, and generally keeping active are very helpful for two reasons. First, they're functions that probably haven't become strongly linked to smoking in the past; hence they're unlikely to elicit strong urges to smoke. Second, regular exercise provides beneficial feedback to you regarding how your body is recovering from the unhealthy effects of smoking. Many ex-smokers who previously thought their decline in physical vigor was just due to aging are astounded to find that they feel much stronger – and younger – once tobacco leaves their lives. They discover, after giving up a product that prematurely ages them and saps their vigor, that they feel rejuvenated.

How to deal with withdrawal symptoms

Most smokers report experiencing some type of withdrawal symptom after they quit. This is the body's way of reacting to the absence of a chemical it has come to depend upon – nicotine.

For most smokers, these symptoms appear within the first twenty-four hours after quitting, peak within one to three days, and then gradually decline over the next week or two, unless some form of nicotine replacement is used. Nicotine-replacement therapy, described in the next chapter, may lessen the initial strength of the withdrawal symptoms, but it stretches out the withdrawal process over a longer period.

Figure 3 (page 55) provides a typical – or average – curve of the strength of most withdrawal symptoms over time. Remember that the course of withdrawal symptoms varies for each individual. But eventually all the symptoms disappear.

Many different physical withdrawal symptoms have been reported, including headache, light-headedness, changes in bowel habits, dry mouth, chest

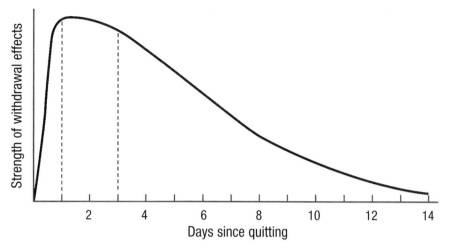

Figure 3: An average or "typical" course of the strength of most withdrawal symptoms following quitting.

pains, throat irritation, increased appetite, and even the development of a cold (despite the fact that on average, ex-smokers develop fewer and much less severe colds than when they smoked). Fortunately, no one has ever reported experiencing them all! In fact, most smokers report just one or two.

A second category of withdrawal symptoms is more psychological; of these, the most common is a craving for a cigarette. Other psychological symptoms include increased irritability, diminished tolerance for frustration, anxiety, difficulty concentrating, labile (easily changing, unstable) moods, and depression.

A third category of withdrawal symptoms involves changes in one's state of arousal or activation level. Some ex-smokers report diminished energy, feelings of fatigue, and more need for sleep, while others have quite opposite symptoms: increased energy, restlessness, and less need for sleep! This seeming contradiction may be related to what is described as the "paradoxical effect of nicotine" on people – the same nicotine that relaxes some people energizes others.

How do you cope with these withdrawal symptoms? The first step is to make sure you realize that these symptoms will gradually diminish and disappear, that no one ever died from these symptoms, and that these bothersome feelings are a small price to pay for avoiding the much more serious and lasting suffering that comes with continued tobacco use. Nicotine replacement or other forms of pharmacological and behavioral treatments may be of benefit here, as well as relaxation and breathing exercises.

A list of common withdrawal symptoms and suggestions for dealing with them is presented in Table 2.

Table 2

**Commonly Reported Withdrawal Symptoms:
Cause, Duration, and Behavior Techniques for Gaining Relief**

Symptom	Cause	Average Duration	Relief
Irritability	Body's craving for nicotine	2-4 weeks	Walks, hot baths, relaxation techniques
Fatigue	Nicotine is a stimulant	2-4 weeks	Take naps; do not push yourself
Insomnia	Nicotine affects brain-wave function, influences sleep patterns; coughing and dreams about smoking are common	1 week	Avoid caffeine after 6 p.m.; relaxation techniques
Cough, dry throat, nasal drip	Body getting rid of mucus, which has blocked airways and restricted breathing	A few days	Cough drops; drink plenty of fluids
Dizziness	Body is getting extra oxygen	1 or 2 days	Take extra caution; change position slowly

Lack of concentration	Body needs time to adjust to not having constant stimulation from nicotine	A few weeks	Plan workload accordingly; avoid additional stress during the first few weeks
Tightness in the chest	Probably due to tension created by body's need for nicotine; may be caused by sore muscles from coughing	A few days	Relaxation techniques, especially deep breathing
Constipation, gas, stomach pain	Intestinal movement decreases for a brief period	1 or 2 weeks	Drink plenty of fluids; add fruits, vegetables, and whole-grain cereals to your diet
Hunger	Craving for a cigarette can be confused with hunger pangs; oral craving, desire for something in the mouth	Up to several weeks	Drink water or low-calorie liquids; be prepared with low-calorie snacks
Craving for cigarette	Withdrawal from nicotine, a strongly addictive drug	Most frequent first 2 or 3 days; can happen occasionally for months or years	Wait out the urge; Cravings last only a few minutes. Distract yourself. Exercise; go for a walk around the block

Adapted from materials provided by the National Cancer Institute.

Coping with urges to smoke

Despite what some former smokers say ("I threw away my cigarettes and never thought about them again!"), probably every smoker who ever quit had to learn to cope with urges to smoke again. Just after you quit, these urges can be substantial and frequent. After all, you're likely to be going through withdrawal as well as encountering a variety of linkages that trigger the urge to smoke.

How can you deal with these urges? First of all, before you quit, you should write on a card the most important reason(s) for quitting. Carry this card at all times, and retrieve and review it whenever a you feel a strong urge to smoke. You should recognize that having cravings is a natural and normal part of the journey to becoming tobacco-free – nothing mysterious or unusual is going on. And each time you stand firm against the craving to smoke (which must be every time!), at least one linkage is being weakened.

In addition, you should realize that these urges do not last long. With the possible exception of the first few days after quitting, most people report that urges to smoke rarely last more than a minute or two. Do *not* tell yourself what some ex-smokers have said to themselves: "How can I live the rest of my life like this?" You *will not* have to live the rest of your life like that, but you may have to be uncomfortable for the next minute or so.

As adults, we've all had to learn to delay the immediate gratification of our needs. So make a positive statement to yourself such as "I have more than enough strength to outlast this annoying urge!"

Then it's time to actively cope with the craving to smoke. Don't simply sit around, waiting for the urge to subside. The longer you remain inactive and think about smoking, the longer your cravings will last. So distract yourself by focusing on something other than your craving. Go for a walk. Get a drink of water. Exercise. Call a friend. Maintaining your new nonsmoking status is an absolute priority, and you need to manage your behavior accordingly. In other words, use some type of coping mechanism.

Soon enough, the cravings will be gone. When this happens, give yourself a pat on the back. Each time you have a craving and don't give in to it – which must be *every time* you have an urge – you've done something really important for yourself, your future, and those you love. You've taken another important step on the journey to becoming tobacco-free. Be proud of yourself for standing firm, and be ever more confident that you will be able to handle the next urge that comes down the road. As long as you stay focused on the journey, you are stronger than any urge, whenever and wherever it occurs.

Chapter 7

Programs, Techniques, and Pills: Ways to Make the Journey Less Bumpy

Many products are advertised as aids to quitting smoking. Most of them have never been proven to be better than a placebo – that is, a sugar pill, with no active medical ingredients. This is not meant to demean the power of placebos. Quite often, if people believe something is going to help them, it actually ends up doing just that! So let's put it this way – the aids described in this chapter have a chance to be useful and have proved themselves more effective than placebos.

But remember: *There are no magic bullets when it comes to quitting.*

The techniques, programs, and pharmacological aids described here are likely to be of some help to some people, but they're no substitute for the planning, patience, and persistence required to successfully complete the journey to a smoke-free life. Persistence includes more than continuing the journey even when you're frustrated; it also means trying new methods and techniques when earlier ones don't seem to help. You must learn from past mistakes and, most of all, refuse to give up on your goal, even if one or more aids to quitting don't meet your expectations.

Education about smoking

Linda was 28 years old when she decided to quit smoking. This decision was quite spontaneous. She was a secretary in a doctor's office, and one day a brightly colored booklet that had been mailed to her boss caught her eye. She opened the booklet and saw some dreadful pictures: a cancerous lung, a cancerous mouth, a lung with emphysema, a brain that had suffered a stroke, and many others – all real photos depicting the consequences of smoking. These images were accompanied by vivid descriptions of the terrible health consequences of smoking.

This booklet had a powerful effect on Linda. "The pictures didn't just frighten me, they disgusted me!" Linda told me later. "What was I doing to my body? How could I continue to do this? I decided to quit right then and there."

Linda marched over to the wastebasket and threw her cigarettes away.

Unfortunately, within a week she was back to smoking again. That week was the longest Linda would go smoke-free until she finally quit years later. The materials she saw quite by accident had made a deep impression on her, but she needed more assistance before she actually quit for good.

At one time, the common belief was that if the public were plainly educated about the incredibly destructive potential of tobacco, smokers would simply quit. And, of course, many have. But education alone is not enough for most people. Many people continue to smoke, despite knowing that tobacco will prematurely age them, rob them of their health, and eventually take their lives. Knowledge of the dangers of smoking may be *necessary* for cessation to take place, but for many it is not *sufficient*.

Instead of focusing just on the negative consequences of smoking, education now highlights the specific, tangible, and positive benefits to be gained by quitting: better health, more attractive appearance, financial savings, better self-image, reduced stress, and less social pressure.

Education about smoking and the process of quitting – a main focus of this book – can be helpful to you. Many smokers have little if any idea of what smoking cessation is all about, which makes the journey toward a smoke-free life more challenging. Hopefully, education can help you avoid pitfalls along the way and make quitting a little easier to accomplish.

Behavior-modification methods

Behavior modification is a broad term that refers to techniques that alter human behavior. Some behavior modifications have been used to help people quit, and these techniques are usually most effective when they are combined with other methods.

One type of behavior modification uses *aversive techniques*. As the term suggests, these techniques aim to arouse aversion, so that the act of smoking becomes quite unpleasant for the smoker. Blowing smoky air into the smoker's face is one example of this method; another is having the smoker inhale so rapidly that nausea occurs. Although studies have shown aversive techniques to be effective, they have fallen out of favor due to their obvious unpleasantness.

Self-monitoring is used in connection with preparing to quit. This involves keeping a record of all smoking in the form of the "smoking diary" described in Chapter 5. In addition to providing useful information about the smoker's linkages, this technique tends to result in a decrease in the number of cigarettes smoked.

Nicotine fading calls for gradually reducing nicotine intake, usually by cutting the number of cigarettes smoked. This is typically used during preparation for quitting, especially with heavy tobacco users who need to get down to a more reasonable level of smoking before they quit entirely. Sometimes, smokers will switch to a "light" or low-tar brand, but research has shown that this has little value, since smokers tend to smoke more low-nicotine cigarettes and thus end up inhaling as much nicotine as before they cut down.

Stimulus control techniques involve eliminating smoking in certain situations as a means of weakening strong linkages. These techniques, which were described in Chapter 5, can be quite useful to the smoker preparing to quit.

Contingency management involves drawing up a contract that rewards subjects for not smoking, or conversely, punishes them for returning to smoking. For example, if you're planning to quit smoking, you may contract to pay someone a deposit that will be returned after you go a specified length of time without smoking, or you may pledge to donate money to an organization you do not like for every cigarette you smoke.

Coping skills can be especially useful in helping people quit and stay that way. Coping skills may be either behavioral (what people do) or cognitive (what they think and tell themselves) when confronted with urges to smoke. They are especially useful in preventing relapse and will be described in greater detail in Chapter 8, which discusses relapse prevention.

Hypnosis and acupuncture

Hypnosis is widely advertised as a method resulting in smoking cessation. But a major problem with hypnosis is the way it is marketed. Some hypnotherapists claim that urges to smoke will magically disappear after a single session. While this sounds fabulous, you must realize there are no magic bullets that make smoking disappear instantly and effortlessly.

Hypnosis helps a person to relax deeply and then become open to suggestions that strengthen the resolve to quit, increase negative feelings toward smoking, and develop more positive feelings toward breathing clean, smoke-free air. Hypnosis can best be viewed as a potentially useful part of a more comprehensive smoking-cessation program. Research bears this out.

Acupuncture possesses attractions similar to those of hypnosis. It promises a relatively effortless and rapid path to quitting. There are many anecdotes about how people quit after a session or two with an acupuncturist. Unfortunately, controlled research studies have not thoroughly validated its effectiveness. The same holds true for laser treatments that are marketed as aids to quitting smoking.

Relaxation and related stress-reduction techniques

Since many smokers say that smoking relaxes them and also report that they feel more tense while they're trying to quit, it's not surprising that techniques that help people relax are popular smoking-cessation techniques.

One relaxation technique is biofeedback, whereby a person learns to control bodily functions such as heart rate or muscle contractions. Similarly, muscle relaxation, yoga, meditation, t'ai chi, guided imagery, breathing exercises, and other approaches are avenues smokers often explore. There is little empirical evidence that these stress-reduction techniques are useful smoking-cessation aids, but when they are combined with other approaches, they do seem to help some people who experience increased tension when they try to kick the habit.

Here is an easy-to-learn relaxation technique that combines visualization and abdominal breathing (breathing that sends air deep into the abdomen instead of to the chest). Sit in a chair, close your eyes, and imagine a brightly colored balloon. While you *slowly* inhale through the nose, direct the air to the lower abdomen, rather than to the chest. During this first breath, imagine the balloon gradually expanding to its full size. Then, after holding the full breath for a few seconds, *slowly* exhale through the mouth and imagine the balloon gradually shrinking toward its original size. Repeat this same sequence for a second breath. Then, during the third and final breath of this exercise, try to visualize the most peaceful, restful setting possible – perhaps you're walking alone at the beach or sitting by a quiet stream, or maybe you're resting on a favorite sofa or easy chair. Whatever scene you choose, it should be the most peaceful and restful place you can think of.

Most people can do this exercise in a minute or less. But learning how to perform abdominal (rather than chest) breathing may require a bit of practice, since we're so used to chest breathing. One way to practice abdominal breathing is simply to lie on your back while breathing. When you're in this position, it's very hard to do chest breathing, since abdominal breathing now happens automatically. You can also maximize and sustain abdominal breathing by placing one hand on the chest and the other hand on the abdomen. If true abdominal breathing occurs, during inhalation the hand on the abdomen should be displaced more than the hand on the chest. Once you get the feel for this type of breathing, you can gradually learn to duplicate this process in other positions, such as sitting.

This quick, simple, portable relaxation technique can be quite useful whenever a craving for a cigarette arises – or just as a means of general stress reduction. Doing it several times each day can actually modify your general stress level over time.

Surprisingly to some, quitting smoking itself is a useful stress-reduction technique! Once an individual undergoes the first few weeks of quitting and most withdrawal symptoms are past, stress levels seem to subside. Six months after quitting, most ex-smokers report experiencing less stress in their lives than they felt when they were smoking, even if they don't use any specific relaxation or stress-reduction techniques.

Pharmacological approaches

For more than fifty years, investigators have been trying to develop a medicine that will help in the cessation process. They explored many medications that blocked the action of nicotine or tried to mimic it, but none was deemed useful, and many products produced disturbing side effects.

During the 1980s, a promising pharmacological approach was born: Nicotine-replacement therapy helps people quit smoking, yet continue to receive nicotine through alternate methods. This let smokers begin to break linkages and modify their other smoking behaviors while continuing to receive nicotine, thus avoiding many of the troublesome withdrawal symptoms and cravings associated with abrupt discontinuation of nicotine.

The first such product was nicotine chewing gum, originally available by prescription only but offered over the counter in 1984. It looks like ordinary chewing gum but contains a nicotine compound designed to slowly release nicotine into the mouth when chewed. The nicotine "patch," sold by prescription in 1991 and available over the counter since 1995, is similar to adhesive bandages and available in different shapes and sizes; larger patches deliver more nicotine through the skin. Applied once daily to the skin and left on for eighteen to twenty-four hours (depending on the brand), the patch delivers a fairly steady dose of nicotine to the person trying to quit.

More recently, other forms of nicotine-replacement therapy were developed: the nicotine inhaler, the nicotine spray, and the nicotine lozenge. The inhaler and spray are available by prescription only, while the lozenge is available over the counter. The inhaler consists of a plastic cylinder containing a cartridge that delivers nicotine when you puff on it. The spray dispenses nicotine from a pump bottle similar to decongestant sprays. Nicotine lozenges look like a hard candy and release nicotine as they slowly dissolve in the mouth.

No one form of nicotine replacement has been shown to outperform the others, and each product has advantages and disadvantages. All supply the body with nicotine doses that are lower than those typically obtained through smoking and seem to ease withdrawal symptoms and cravings for nicotine. The nicotine gum must be chewed properly, or it will deliver uncomfortably high doses of nicotine. The spray can be irritating to the nose and cause a hot, peppery feeling along with watery eyes, runny nose, coughing, and sneezing. The nicotine inhaler needs to be used frequently throughout the day to achieve its desired effect; mouth and throat irritation are its most common side effects. Heartburn, hiccups, and nausea are side effects that have been reported with the nicotine lozenge. The nicotine patch can produce skin irritations where the patch is placed.

But the nicotine patch does have one distinct advantage: ease of discontinuance. With the other forms of nicotine replacement – gum, inhaler, spray, and lozenge – many people have difficulty stopping their nicotine replacement and continue using it long after they should stop. This has rarely been reported as a problem with the nicotine patch, probably because the patch delivers nicotine more slowly than do the other forms of replacement and hence provides no nicotine "buzz."

But keep this in mind: Although turning to nicotine replacement for long periods is certainly better than smoking – the user doesn't receive the dozens of poisons and carcinogens contained in tobacco smoke – nicotine is still a known poison that may have serious long-term effects on the body, especially the heart.

The first non-nicotine medication approved by the Food and Drug Administration for use in smoking cessation was bupropion. Sold under the brand name of Zyban, it is a prescription medication that comes in a pill form. It does not contain nicotine. Zyban's history is interesting. Smokers who happened to be users of the antidepressant medication Wellbutrin (bupropion hydrochloride) often reported a diminished desire for cigarettes. Further testing revealed that the drug was useful in reducing both withdrawal symptoms and cravings for nicotine. It was renamed Zyban and marketed as an aid to smoking cessation in 1997. Unlike the nicotine-replacement aids to smoking cessation, Zyban comes with a recommendation that the smoker start using it at least a week before quitting.

In May 2006, the FDA approved a second non-nicotine medication intended to help cigarette smokers stop smoking. Brand-named Chantix, varenicline tartrate reportedly acts at sites in the brain affected by nicotine and may help those who wish to give up smoking in two ways: by providing some nicotine effects to ease the withdrawal symptoms and by blocking the effects of nicotine from cigarettes if the individuals who are trying to quit start smoking again. As with Zyban, it is recommended that the smoker start using Chantix tablets one week before quitting.

Of all medications that assist in the quitting process, nicotine gum and the nicotine patch are the most widely used. Their heavy usage may be related in part to the high profitability they provide to the companies that manufacture them, together with the ease with which they are delivered. They are heavily marketed and widely advertised as "doubling the long-term quit rates." This may be true when compared with minimal interventions (such as physicians urging their patients to quit but doing nothing more), but these and all pharmacological aids are much more likely to prove useful when combined with other methods such as smoking-cessation programs that employ behavior-modification techniques.

Smoking-cessation groups

Self-help groups for smokers trying to quit smoking provide an atmosphere in which people can support and learn from one another. Just as it's usually more pleasant and reassuring for people to travel with others to a far-off land than to travel alone, so, too, it is with the journey to a smoke-free life. Groups that use a combination of treatments – like the multimodal approaches described on page 68 – are most likely to be successful. Not all smokers making quit attempts choose to attend group cessation programs, but those who do are likely to find the experience helpful. Many smoking-cessation group programs that use behavior-modification techniques report the highest rates of successful quitting among their members.

Some communities have a Nicotine Anonymous group that holds regular meetings. These groups apply the twelve-step principles of Alcoholics Anonymous to the addiction of smoking.

For information on how to contact Nicotine Anonymous and other smoking-cessation groups, and a listing of other helpful websites, see Appendices 2 and 3.

Telephone "quit lines" and helpful websites

Most states run some type of free telephone "quit line," which links callers with trained counselors. These specialists help plan a quit method that fits each person's unique smoking pattern. Telephone counseling is also more convenient than support programs for many people because they can remain at home; also, telephone counseling doesn't require transportation or child care, and it's available nights and weekends.

Counselors may recommend a combination of methods including medications, coping strategies, self-help brochures, and/or a network of family and friends. Callers' programs are often individualized. Although various states use different quit lines, there is a national toll-free telephone number that connects callers to the quit lines in their states: 1-800-QUIT NOW (1-800-784-8669). This number connects the caller to the National Network of Tobacco Cessation Quitlines.

There is also a variety of online websites that provide cessation assistance. Some of these provide live interaction with a smoking-cessation specialist. Some are free; others charge a fee. A list of some of the better-known sites may be found in Appendix 3.

Multimodal approaches

Because there is no single, most effective approach to smoking cessation and because different individuals benefit from different treatment approaches, a multimodal (or multicomponent) plan of smoking cessation seems most useful. These plans may combine several methods: education, behavior modification, pharmaceuticals, hypnosis, group support, relaxation, and stress management. Some plans even include a physical exercise component. Multimodal programs typically outperform any single treatment modality and achieve the highest rates of smoking cessation.

Some of the better-known multimodal smoking-cessation programs are sponsored by major health agencies. Among these are the American Lung Association's "Freedom from Smoking Program" and the American Cancer Society's "Make Yours a Fresh Start Family," a program that helps health-care providers learn how to counsel pregnant women and mothers who want to stop smoking.

Which approach for me?

By now, it should be clear that there is no single technique that works best for everyone. Perhaps this is why multimodal approaches that use a variety of methods typically produce the highest cessation rates. Group approaches tend to be a bit more effective than individual approaches, and pharmaceuticals such as nicotine-replacement therapies, Zyban, and Chantix increase program effectiveness for many smokers.

As recommended earlier, you should make at least one serious attempt to quit on your own before turning to any specific programs. If you don't achieve success, then turning to a telephone quit line or an interactive website could be an appropriate step. If you need still more assistance, a multimodal program – either group or individual – would be a realistic next step.

Sometimes smokers need to repeat and redouble their efforts before they achieve success. If this is your experience, it might mean turning to a group if you first took an individual approach or vice versa. It doesn't matter how many detours or different modes of transportation you take on your journey to a smoke-free life, so long as you reach that final destination. A healthful, smoke-free life is truly the Promised Land, and it's worth many times the amount of effort needed to reach it!

Chapter 8

Maintaining a Smoke-Free Lifestyle

Mark Twain, the noted American humorist, is credited with saying, "Giving up smoking is the easiest thing in the world. I should know; I've done it a thousand times." What Twain was really talking about was not quitting but the maintenance of quitting.

Almost every smoker has quit for at least a short period. Some have quit for only a few hours. Many have quit for weeks, months, even years. They appeared to achieve their goal of a smoke-free life, but then something happened and they experienced a relapse.

Simply put, they returned to smoking.

A relapse usually begins with an impulsive, poorly thought-out decision to have a cigarette. Even though most smokers will tell you they know (at some level) that having a single cigarette is likely to lead to a full-blown resumption of their smoking, they somehow blot out that knowledge and have one anyway. And once that happens, the lower brain centers (those portions of the brain that were previously hooked on nicotine) take over.

So the key to preventing relapse is to strengthen the higher brain centers (the parts of our brain that are involved in rational thinking and planning) so much that the lower brain centers *cannot* take over, even temporarily. That takeover is what happened to Lila when she relapsed.

Lila started smoking when she was in college. At that time, in the early 1950s, smoking was the fashionable thing to do. In her college dining room, especially at lunch and dinner, free packs containing four cigarettes were frequently distributed, much as an upscale hotel chain today might place wrapped chocolates on the pillows of its guests.

One beautiful spring day, Lila and her best friend, Marge, had just finished dinner and were not looking forward to a long evening of studying in a stuffy library. Marge had an idea: Skip the library on this balmy spring evening and go for a walk. Marge also suggested that they pick up the free cigarette packs and the matches thoughtfully placed beside them. Neither Lila nor Marge smoked, but many of their friends did, and they frequently gave their samples to their friends. So off they went into the beautiful evening with their free tobacco in hand.

Little did they know how that evening would change their lives!

After about fifteen minutes of walking, they ran into a group of their classmates. Nearly all were smoking. The group included several boys, one of whom had seemed quite interested in Marge (and vice versa). But tonight, Bob seemed to pointedly ignore Marge, something that disturbed her a good deal. She didn't outwardly show that she was upset, but Lila sensed it immediately. When the group walked on, leaving Lila and Marge alone, Marge burst into tears. They sat together on a bench to discuss the situation. Marge reached into her purse for a tissue to dry her tears. She couldn't find the tissues, but she did see the pack of four cigarettes. In an impulsive moment, she picked up the pack, ripped off the cellophane, took out a cigarette, and lit up.

What happened next seemed almost hilarious, but in the long run turned out to be quite sad. Marge took her first puff and began to choke and cough. Her reaction was so different from the seemingly sophisticated smoking of the classmates she had just been with that she began to laugh – and her tears stopped flowing. Lila, who was sensitive to her friend's feelings, was relieved to see Marge laughing instead of crying. Perhaps motivated by a desire to share a moment of closeness with her friend, she said, "Give me one of those!" and lit up her own cigarette. She, too, began coughing and sputtering. Then they laughed together. "That darn Bob drove us to smoking!" Marge exclaimed.

After the first few puffs, their bodies seemed to adapt to the irritating smoke. They also were feeling the "buzz" produced by the nicotine's rapid ascent into their brains. They sat on the bench, watching a lovely spring sunset and discussing Marge's situation with Bob. "Might as well finish off this pack," Marge said. Each had her second cigarette of the evening, but this time, there was no choking and coughing. In fact, as they finished these cigarettes, they began to enjoy the heady sensation of nicotine.

The next day they smoked again, even though the "crisis" that prompted their actions the night before had been resolved. Bob actually called Marge, and the two became a couple again.

Both Lila and Marge continued smoking until Lila quit about twenty years later. The two women remained lifelong friends; they saw each other at college reunions and occasionally visited each other, though they lived many hundreds of miles apart. Through Lila had quit, Marge kept smoking, and sadly enough her smoking was a factor in Lila's relapse – just as Marge had been an influence in Lila's beginning to smoke.

Lila's relapse occurred at Marge's house. About forty years after they graduated from college, Lila came to visit. The trip had been unusually stressful. Marge lived in a large city, and Lila had driven through some horrible rush-hour traffic to get there. But now they were together again, relaxing and having a glass of wine outdoors in a splendid summer evening.

"The setting was perfect. The moon was full and shining brightly, the summer breeze was warm and soft, the wine was delicious, and I was so glad to be there with my friend," Lila told me later. "Then Marge took out a cigarette and jokingly offered one to me. I'm sure she never thought I'd take it, since I had been on her back about quitting for years. But something came over me, and for a split second that cigarette seemed so inviting. So I said yes, and before she had a chance to retract her offer the cigarette was in my mouth and I was lighting it with the lighter she had placed on the table by the wine bottle. I figured that after all these years with no smoking and not having any desire to have one, I was safe."

Although her reaction to that first cigarette was in many ways reminiscent of the very first cigarette she had taken more than forty years earlier – she choked, coughed, and sputtered – she also felt that nicotine buzz, which she remembered even though she hadn't thought about it in years. And just like her reaction after that spring night at college so many years earlier, Lila smoked the next day and the next, and within a week was back to the same level of smoking she'd been at two decades ago, before she quit.

Five years later, following some serious health changes and strong admonitions from her physician, she quit again – she hoped for good.

Lila's story illustrates some important truths about maintenance and relapse. Perhaps the most important principle is this: Regardless of the lack of any conscious desire for a cigarette, no former smoker is ever *totally* safe from an impulse to smoke. In an unguarded moment, an urge to smoke may emerge without warning. You must know that this can happen and be ready to deal with the urge when it arises.

Regardless of the length of time – days, weeks, months, years – since your last cigarette, reintroducing tobacco (even just *one* cigarette!) can lead to a full-blown relapse. Why? Because your brain is permanently and irrevocably altered in such a way as to make full-blown resumption of tobacco use virtually automatic. That new cigarette has invisible but powerful connections to the hundreds and thousands of other cigarettes you smoked before it.

Perhaps an analogy will help illustrate this concept. In the southwestern United States, especially in the deserts, there are numerous arroyos (dry creek beds or gulches that fill with water after a heavy rain). If you come upon one of those dry gulches during dry weather, it appears to be a harmless-looking indentation in the landscape similar to a dried-up riverbed. But when a sizable rain occurs, that arroyo can quickly become a raging river, ready to swallow any unsuspecting animal, human being, or automobile in its path. The landscape that contains an arroyo has been permanently altered in a fashion that makes it ready to receive and carry water in large amounts, regardless of how long it has been dry.

Similarly, the human brain is permanently altered by nicotine addiction. Just as the arroyo lies ready to receive rainfall no matter how long it has been since the last rain, so the brain is always ready to receive nicotine no matter how long it has been since the last cigarette. But there's one important difference between the two. When the rain subsides and the land dries, the arroyo automatically returns to its dry condition. The human brain, however, continues to crave nicotine and to resist its absence. The quitting process has to be initiated all over again for the brain to "dry out."

Maintenance: What it's all about

A dictionary definition of the word "maintenance" is "activity involved in maintaining something in good working order."

We maintain our automobiles so they'll continue to transport us reliably from one place to another. It may not take a lot of time and effort to maintain today's cars, but if we skip maintenance altogether, they will break down. Similarly, after you quit smoking, you need to keep your quitting in good working order.

For most former smokers, this doesn't take a lot of effort. But few things in life are maintenance-free, and quitting smoking is certainly not one of them. It's sad but true that most people who quit smoking are likely to relapse within a year. Even more disappointing are the findings that some ex-smokers relapse, as Lila did, many years after they've quit.

The basic rule of quitting

In most things, people don't need to be perfect to do just fine. We don't have to be perfect parents, perfect workers, or perfect partners to succeed. Doing well is usually good enough. We expect to make mistakes once in a while, learn from our mistakes, and go on. Of course, making too many mistakes and not learning from them can cause real problems.

Here's an example: Let's say that Bob is trying to lose a few pounds. He realizes that he has a bowl of ice cream almost every night while he watches television, so he chooses to eliminate that activity in pursuit of his goal. He does fine for about two weeks and then in a moment of weakness remembers the chocolate ice cream in the freezer and succumbs to temptation. He has a bowl. Later he views this action with regret and promises himself that he won't repeat his ice-cream binge the next night. It may take a little more effort that next night not to have a bowl of ice cream, but he does it without much difficulty. He had weakened the habit of having ice cream in the evening, so a single slip didn't lead to full-blown resumption of his ice-cream-eating behavior.

Meanwhile, Bob's wife, Helen, quits smoking about the same time as Bob eliminates his bowl of ice cream in the evening. A few weeks later, while she's watching a movie on television in which several characters are smoking, she decides to have a cigarette. Unfortunately for her, she hadn't thrown away all her cigarettes when she quit – she left a few cigarettes in a pack at the bottom of one of her kitchen drawers; now she remembers them, grabs one, and lights up. Later she too makes a promise to herself not to repeat this action.

Unlike her husband's experience with his evening ice cream, Helen finds herself wanting another cigarette not long after she has finished the first one. And the next day, when she rises in the morning, smoking is on her mind. It remains on her mind the entire day. The next evening, while she's watching television again, the urge to have another cigarette becomes really strong. It takes a lot of effort for her not to go to the kitchen drawer. At last she finds herself unable to muster sufficient energy to resist, so she has another cigarette, and the process that began the day before is strengthened. Cigarettes have reentered Helen's life; she becomes an active smoker again. She has begun a process that sooner or later will lead to a full-blown resumption of her smoking.

What's the difference here between Bob breaking his ice-cream habit and Helen staying off cigarettes? Simply put, while ice cream can certainly be habit-forming, it is not addictive in the true sense of the word. Smoking, on the other hand, is *truly addictive*. And addictions operate by distinctly different rules. As with most things in life, when you set out to break a habit, perfection is not required – just a fine sustained effort. But to successfully break an addiction, a bit of perfection is required. Just as an alcoholic cannot have a drink from time to time and still remain "on the wagon," you cannot have a cigarette from time to time and still remain a nonsmoker. Indeed, many experts assert that nicotine is considerably more addictive than alcohol or heroin. Even if you haven't had a real urge to smoke for a very long time, as Lila hadn't, any urge that you don't resist successfully is very likely to lead to a full-blown resumption of your entire smoking pattern, no matter how much time has elapsed since you quit.

Unfortunately, this kind of relapse happens much too often with ex-smokers. So how do you successfully resist relapsing?

"Giving up smoking is the easiest thing in the world. I know, because I've done it thousands of times."

Basically, you need to have the right frame of mind about smoking. Many, many individuals who have quit think of themselves as having broken a habit, just as Bob did with his evening bowl of ice cream. Bob never thought of himself as giving up ice cream forever; he simply wanted to stop eating it every evening. In the back of his mind, he knew he could and would have ice cream from time to time without erasing the progress he'd made in eliminating it from his evening schedule. Similarly, too many ex-smokers think that the day will come when they can have a cigarette or two without going back to full-blown smoking. Many even envision themselves becoming "social smokers" at some future date, having a cigarette now and then but never becoming a regular smoker again.

Nothing could be further from the truth!

Once you become a regular smoker, the addictive process kicks in. This means that you cannot turn back time to a point before your smoking began. Your brain has become irreversibly altered and is ready to receive and react to nicotine, just as that arroyo in the desert has been permanently altered to receive rain. Yes, there are social smokers who, for some unknown reason, don't seem to get hooked on nicotine. These folks are called "chippers." They can go for long periods without smoking, only to have a few cigarettes on certain occasions without jeopardizing their status. (Yet some of these chippers do eventually develop full-blown smoking patterns.) But for virtually all other smokers, becoming an occasional puffer is simply not an option. Indeed, the basic rule of quitting is quite simple and straightforward: *"Smoking is no longer an option in my life!"*

There can be no "fine-print" exceptions to this basic rule. No exceptions, even if you lose a loved one. No exceptions, even if your career takes a major hit. No exceptions for massive financial reversals. No exceptions whatsoever! If your contract with yourself contains even a single exception, it's entirely likely that at some point in life, the condition(s) represented by that exception will recur – and so will regular smoking.

When an urge to smoke arises, as it did when Helen was watching that movie on TV, you must simply tell yourself, "Smoking is not an option in my life." Then plug in some type of coping mechanism to deal with that urge to smoke. Helen could have switched channels, turned off her television entirely, gone for a walk, or engaged in another behavior. She could even have retrieved her cigarettes (which she shouldn't have kept in the first place), soaked them with water, and thrown them in the garbage, where they belonged. Instead, she took the one action that was prohibited – she had a cigarette! This led to a quite predictable and speedy return to smoking. Helen had neglected to maintain her quitting properly. And so she relapsed.

Remote linkages and relapse

Any time a behavior (such as smoking) occurs repeatedly in a particular situation (such as driving a car), a bond between the two is established. This bond is called a linkage, and many linkages are so strong, a smoker will desire a cigarette in a certain situation even if he's not experiencing nicotine depletion at that moment. For example, simply entering an automobile elicits a desire to smoke in many smokers.

When you quit smoking and live your life as a nonsmoker, you gradually weaken and eventually break the regular linkages you encounter in your daily lives. Linkages that are rarely experienced are called remote linkages, and they can present you with a special challenge.

Let's go back to Lila's story. She had seen Marge only a few times since she quit smoking. And for Lila, Marge certainly was a smoking buddy – indeed, many years earlier Lila and Marge had started the habit together, which is one of the most powerful linkages in existence. So it's not surprising that for Lila, Marge represented a remote linkage – an association with smoking that she hadn't completely broken yet. To make matters even worse, alcohol was involved, and, since she continued to smoke, Marge was a potential source of tobacco supply for Lila.

Experiences with remote linkages are likely to arise for every ex-smoker at one time or another, simply because it isn't possible to break all linkages with smoking in a short time. The first time you face a real-life crisis after you quit smoking, remote linkages are likely to appear – and with them, urges to smoke. High school and college reunions are another potential source of remote linkages, since they're likely to include old "smoking buddies," whom you may not have seen at all since you quit. Every time something unusual occurs after you quit smoking, from the first summer picnic to the first New Year's celebration, you must be on guard and ready to cope with urges to smoke. Even the time of year, such as the day of the first snowstorm or the first really nice spring day, may turn out to be a remote linkage.

A class reunion can be a source of remote linkages and thus be likely to generate strong urges to smoke and be a potential for relapse.

These urges may be quite powerful, but usually they're short-lived. With some practice, you can develop the skill to predict many of these remote linkages. But no matter how skillful you become in predicting possible remote linkages, at least a few of them are likely to blindside you by coming out of the blue. However, whether you anticipate them or not, you must cope with and resist any urges to smoke elicited by remote linkages. *Smoking is not an option. If you smoke even one cigarette, relapse is virtually inevitable.*

Alcohol and relapse

For complex reasons that are not entirely clear, the association between alcohol and smoking is very strong for most smokers. A minority of smokers, of course, don't drink alcohol at all, and for these individuals there is no association between the two behaviors. But for most smokers, drinking and smoking seem to go together. In fact, many young people begin smoking and drinking at about the same time. Perhaps this is one reason that the two activities can become so closely associated.

There may be other reasons for the strong association between tobacco and alcohol. Duke University Medical Center researchers have found that even small amounts of alcohol boost the pleasurable effects of nicotine, inducing people to smoke more when they're drinking alcoholic beverages. In any event, when most smokers have a drink, there's definitely an accompanying urge to smoke. So when you quit, it's imperative that in the beginning of your quitting journey you drink very little – or better yet, not at all. Not only are alcoholic beverages strongly linked with smoking, but alcohol has a definite tendency to turn off or damp down the higher brain centers. Many, many cases of early relapse occur when the new ex-smoker settles in with his friends and has a few drinks.

After a few weeks, if you're like most smokers who have quit, you will gradually become able to begin light drinking – no more than one or two drinks at a time. (If you experience strong urges to smoke while you're drinking, you should immediately stop drinking and leave the bar or party!) As time passes, the linkage between smoking and alcohol weakens and eventually breaks altogether. But as in Lila's case, alcohol imbibed in a situation like a visit with an old friend unquestionably contributes to urges to smoke and plays a definite role in relapse. Alcohol can interfere with clear thinking and planning, and all too often it makes smokers forget their "game plans" (see below).

Coffee and other caffeinated beverages such as colas may also be associated with smoking. In the early stages of quitting, their presence may evoke in some people a strong desire to smoke. For this reason, in the early stages of quitting, people should not linger over coffee or other beverages containing caffeine. Fortunately, these drinks do not interfere with useful "game plans" for smoke-free maintenance the way alcohol does.

Game plans for staying quit

Urges to smoke can still occur years after people have stopped smoking. Just as successful competitors in sports have a plan for dealing with situations they're likely to face, you should have some type of game plan to deal with these urges. Game plans may be highly useful, highly destructive, or somewhere in between. Let's start with a highly destructive game plan, one that could result in relapse.

Al quit smoking about a year before he relapsed. He had a strong urge to smoke while attending his company's holiday party, where a lot of his co-workers were still smoking. A strong urge to smoke hit him within a few minutes. Making the situation particularly dangerous, of course, was the ready availability of cigarettes from his former smoking buddies.

Al's first mistake was what he said to himself. Psychologists would call what Al said a faulty self-statement. He told himself, "I've a gone a whole year without smoking, and I still have the urge to smoke. I can't live the rest of my life like this!" Al's statement was distorting; if he'd taken an accurate look at what the past year had been like since he quit, he'd have noted that he'd gone weeks with hardly a thought about smoking. And his statement "I can't live the rest of my life like this!" was totally erroneous. Of course he couldn't live the rest of his life with that type of craving for cigarettes – who could? But he and any other ex-smoker could certainly live the *next few minutes* without giving in to the urge to smoke.

The second mistake Al made involved his behavior. Instead of walking away from smokers when his urge to smoke first hit, he stayed with them. And if walking away hadn't worked, he should have left the party altogether. *For an ex-smoker, remaining smoke-free must be among the very highest priorities in life.* Unfortunately, if you go back to smoking, someday a high priority in your life is likely to be the devastating health effects of smoking.

So Al stayed at the party, had a few drinks, kept spending time with friends who were still smoking, and kept having urges to smoke. Eventually he bummed a cigarette, then another and another. Within a week, he was back to smoking about a pack per day. Al's game plan was clearly faulty, and it led to relapse. He felt awful about himself and what he had done, and eventually he had to go through the entire quitting process again.

A typical helpful game plan is for you to note that an urge has occurred, assess the nature of the situation (often it will be a stressful or unusual one), and then decide on a positive plan of action. Such a plan of action typically involves your:

- Telling yourself that such urges to smoke, even when they occur long after quitting, are both normal and to be expected
- Telling yourself that most of these urges will last only a few seconds, or at most a few minutes
- Using some type of coping strategy to deal with the situation

After the game plan has worked, you should give yourself a pat on the back. Others present may not even know that an internal struggle was going on or that you employed a constructive game plan and succeeded in remaining smoke-free. But you should recognize the victory and be proud of the effort. For you – and all ex-smokers – there is little, if anything, more important in life than remaining smoke-free. It is by far the most precious gift you can give yourself. Whenever you have protected that gift by success-fully deflecting the urge to smoke, you have every right in the world to be very proud!

Relapse crises

Virtually all smokers who quit experience urges to smoke from time to time. Many of these urges are clearly associated with the various links to smoking that once existed in their lives. Most of these urges are short-lived and read-ily managed. But now and then, some ex-smokers go through what is called a "relapse crisis."

A dictionary definition of crisis is "an unstable situation of extreme dan-ger or difficulty." Apply that definition to relapse. The result is a strong, seemingly overwhelming desire to return to smoking. In other words, a relapse crisis is much, much more than a simple urge to have a cigarette – its intensity is much stronger than a simple urge. There is a definite sensation of strong craving involved. A relapse crisis has a much longer duration than an urge and may last for many minutes – or even for hours. It's as if some ex-smokers cannot get the thought of smoking out their minds!

Many different factors can lead to relapse crises. Psychologist Saul Shiffman and his colleagues have done much pioneering work in this area. In a study that analyzed calls to a smoking-cessation hotline, it was found that over two-thirds of the callers experiencing relapse crises were feeling a negative emotion; anxiety was the most commonly reported emotion, followed by anger, frustration, and depression. However, one-third of the relapse crises were linked to positive mood states and were frequently precipitated by the presence of other smokers, eating food, and drinking alcohol. Interpersonal conflict and social pressure were also factors for some.

Debbie had an altogether different reason for undergoing a relapse crisis that occurred about six months after she quit. "I was going along so nicely, hardly even thinking about smoking, and then I had this overpowering urge to have a cigarette that just would not go away. It just came out of the blue, with no warning!" she says. "It lasted for hours – and eventually for days."

Debbie's situation was a bit unusual. She had developed a complex and dangerous health condition that made it absolutely necessary for her to quit.

Although her husband continued to smoke, she quit with relatively little effort and was extremely happy about it, especially since her health had improved almost immediately.

Then, about six months after she quit, she was hit with a powerful case of the flu. "What a time for those darned urges to smoke to come flooding back to me!" she says.

At first, there appeared to be no clear explanation as to why Debbie experienced a relapse crisis when she developed the flu. But further study revealed some interesting facts. Certainly she was experiencing negative emotions – she had endured a lot of poor health over the years, and getting ill now, when she was feeling so well since quitting smoking, was a real disappointment.

But another influence became clear that might have been of even greater importance. In the past, when Debbie became ill, she'd try to get out of bed and be as active as possible. But because she lacked energy and felt terrible, she often spent long hours on the couch in her family room – smoking! In other words, being ill and spending long hours on her couch was a strong smoking linkage for Debbie. Since this was the first time she'd gotten ill since quitting smoking, it was also the first time she experienced this linkage. And since she continued to stay on the couch for hours at a time, she was continually exposed to the linkage. Debbie's relapse crisis seemed to be clearly related to a strong remote linkage between smoking, being ill, and spending time on her couch. Indeed, when she experimented with spending time in bed (a place where she never had smoked), her relapse crisis spontaneously evaporated.

Coping mechanisms for avoiding relapse

If you've formed some type of active coping mechanism, when you're faced with temptations to smoke, you're likely to do better than those who have no game plan. Coping mechanisms fall into two categories:

- Behavioral coping skills (what you do)
- Cognitive coping skills (what you think)

Examples of behavioral skills include eating or drinking something (preferably, nothing too fattening), distracting yourself with an activity, leaving a situation entirely, engaging in some type of physical activity, or engaging in relaxation, meditation, or another form of de-stressing behavior. Cognitive coping skills include reminding yourself of the positive health consequences of remaining smoke-free, thinking about the negative effect on your health of going back to smoking, thinking about how others might react if you relapse, and mental distraction.

Motivation to quit smoking and determination to stay on the journey to a smoke-free life are incredibly important factors in quitting smoking and are good examples of willpower. But willpower is not passively or stoically sitting by and doing nothing while waiting for the urge to pass. Active behavioral and cognitive coping responses are much more effective.

Because so many urges to smoke seem to emerge in response to external stimuli (such as Al's holiday party), escape may be an especially useful tool. Changing the situation if at all possible (for example, stop talking to a former smoking buddy when your urge to smoke arises) often results in a complete end to the urge. And when the urge to light up comes from within, perhaps in response to a strong negative emotion such as anger or anxiety, then try another coping mechanism. Distraction (engaging in a different activity and/or specifically trying to change one's thought patterns) is often a very useful device for coping with such urges.

One very common coping mechanism is eating or drinking something, preferably something light in sugar and calories. Sugarless gum is recommended, since it stimulates the mouth but provides only a few calories. Also potentially helpful is engaging in some type of physical activity, such as going for a walk or climbing a few flights of stairs. A mental coping mechanism is reminding yourself of the positive benefits of quitting or the negative consequences of returning to smoking. If the urge to smoke still persists, try calling on social support from a trusted (nonsmoking) person.

If all else fails, use the simple coping mechanism of *delay* – wait twenty minutes before making any decision about going back to smoking. Urges to smoke will go away whether you smoke or not; however, if you smoke, there is a real risk that smoking will quickly and powerfully reenter your life. Delay provides time for your higher mental processes to reestablish control over the lower brain centers, where the addiction to nicotine lives.

Most of all, when faced with either simple urges to smoke or genuine long-lasting relapse crises, you must remind yourself of the basic rule: *Smoking is not an option in my life.*

This may indeed be the most valuable coping skill. If this basic rule is deeply ingrained in your thinking, there's no room for any internal debate over whether to have a cigarette. Unfortunately, once ex-smokers get caught up in any type of inner struggle about whether to have a cigarette, it's likely to be only a matter of time before they make the decision to light up. There are many, many choices available for someone dealing with any situation in life that arises from an urge or temptation to smoke. For you as an ex-smoker, smoking is no longer an option. It's your responsibility to select one (or more than one) coping strategy to avoid a relapse.

Case closed!

What about "slips?"

Throughout this book, the emphasis has been on quitting and remaining smoke-free. In theory, just saying no to smoking is the easiest and most direct way to maintain a smoke-free life. But we are human, and not everyone is able to live life in such a black-and-white way. Sometimes a relapse crisis occurs that is so powerful, even a committed quitter gives in and has a cigarette or two. Some people have reported that in an unguarded moment, a cigarette seems to have just appeared in their mouths!

What if you have a "slip" or "lapse"? The answer is simple: *Don't let a "lapse" become a "relapse"!*

First, tell yourself that having a slip is not the end of the world. Quitting smoking is a journey. Just because you take an unplanned detour, it doesn't mean that all is lost and the journey is over. Some people slip and have a cigarette once or twice, but quickly get back on track. So if you do slip, it doesn't mean that you've failed. It's critically important *not* to label yourself a failure. To do so could well evoke a sense of despair, which will make it much more likely that you will smoke again and again, and soon be back to regular smoking. Instead, look at a slip or lapse as a learning experience.

There are no failures on the journey to a smoke-free life, except for those who quit trying entirely. If you slip, analyze the situation that led to the slip. Ask yourself these questions:

- What was happening at the time?

- Was it the external situation that led to the slip?

- Was it some internal state – say, a feeling or thought?

Usually, with a little detective work, answers to these questions become apparent. Then, analyze how the situation could have been handled differently. For example, could you have left the situation or become engaged in some type of delay or coping mechanism until the urge to smoke dissipated?

You need to make a strong mental note of this so that if similar situations – and urges – arise in the future, there will be a plan for dealing with them.

If you've relapsed and smoked just a few cigarettes, treat this slip as a temporary setback. Stop smoking immediately! Throw away all your cigarettes, and strengthen your inner resolve not to slip again. If you've gone back to smoking several cigarettes a day for more than a couple of days – well, don't conclude that you failed, unless you've stopped trying. Pick a new quit date, learn from your mistakes, and be even stronger the next time. Stay with the journey!

Although most travelers want to reach their destination in the most organized and predictable way possible, getting there is the crucial part. In the long run, whether their journey involved a detour is inconsequential. Similarly, people who have a slip must pick themselves up and brush themselves off, analyze and learn from their lapse, and get back to their journey. It may take a little longer to reach the marvelous destination of a smoke-free life, but the journey is still worth it.

Chapter 9

Helping Others Become Smoke-Free

Frank and Martha were a delightful couple. They'd been married for more than fifty years, and it was instantly obvious even to a casual observer that they were very much in love. But they were also facing a dreadful crisis and were not doing well at working together to take care of their emergency. That pressing necessity was Frank's health.

Frank had been a light smoker for many years. He rarely smoked more than five cigarettes a day, but he'd been smoking at that relatively low level for nearly sixty years. He assumed that because he smoked fewer cigarettes than any smoker he knew – cigarettes that were low in tar and nicotine at that – he would be unaffected by the ravages smoking inflicts on health. And so he was, until a routine physical exam discovered a spot on his lung that was later diagnosed as lung cancer.

Tragically, it is often true with lung cancer that once symptoms of the disease appear, the likelihood of recovery is slim. But Frank was one of the lucky ones who had no active symptoms of lung cancer – his doctor said so immediately after Frank was diagnosed – and once his cancerous tumor was removed, he'd be fine. Provided, of course, that he stopped smoking, which was essential to prevent the development of additional tumors. This health concern was the basis of the crisis between Frank and Martha.

Martha had never smoked, but she'd been relatively tolerant of Frank's smoking over their many years together. He was a considerate smoker, never smoking in their house or car when Martha was present. She had made some half-hearted efforts over the years to persuade Frank to quit, but her suggestions always fell on deaf ears. He made excuses related to his low level of smoking and apparently robust health. All that, of course, changed with his diagnosis of lung cancer. She badly wanted Frank to quit smoking and told him she would help him any way she could.

After many years of industrious work, Frank and Martha were retired. They were enjoying these years more than any others in their lives, and they wanted to extend this happiness as long as possible. After Frank's successful lung surgery, the only obstacle to their continued sweet life together was his persistent smoking. No matter what the doctors said, no matter how much his children and grandchildren tried to reason with him, Frank continued to smoke. Yes, he agreed in principle that he should quit, but he somehow never got around to it. Martha's encouragement, pleading, and frustrated lectures to him were not enough to turn the tide. Frank continued to smoke.

Martha decided she would take matters into her own hands and become a one-woman "smoking-police" unit. She would find and destroy his smoking materials wherever they existed, so that he'd have nothing to smoke and would have to quit. She began searching everywhere, inside and outside their house. And she was successful, to a point. She found cigarettes hidden on the back porch, in the trunk of their car, under their deck, even inside the cabinet of their barbecue grill! She approached him with the results of her "raids" and destroyed his cigarettes in front of him. He smiled, shook his head, thanked her for trying to help him, and then chided her for "wasting money by destroying perfectly good cigarettes."

Despite her best intentions, her raids had no effect on his smoking, except to make him ever more inventive in hiding his stockpiles of cigarettes. Like a clever squirrel burying his acorns for the winter ahead, Frank found new and creative places to stash his smokes. When Martha discovered them, he found even more ingenious places. So his smoking continued – and so did his risk of a recurrence of lung cancer.

What was going wrong here?

The problem, of course, is obvious. Martha was quite committed to Frank's quitting, but Frank was not. He understood his wife's concerns, he agreed with them, he wanted to quit, *but he never committed himself to quitting.* So, while Martha's intentions were good, the results were not. Instead of Frank quitting, he and his wife became locked in a silly game of search and destroy, in which she meticulously sought to capture his supply of cigarettes and he creatively found new places to hide his treasure. Her war on his "drugs" (tobacco) just was not working.

The story of Frank and Martha does have a happy ending. Eventually he committed himself to quitting, joined a group cessation program, and quit. Before he quit, Martha was persuaded to give up her self-appointed role as the "smoking-police" woman, since the responsibility for quitting *had* to reside with her husband. She could still be supportive of him throughout the quitting process (which she was), but it was up to him – not her – to end his smoking.

Some specific do's and don'ts

How can you help others in your life quit smoking? No single answer fits everyone perfectly. A lot has to do with your relationship with the smoker. For example, there are things a grandchild might say to a grandparent about smoking that a spouse should not say to a spouse. But here are some general principles.

1) Don't threaten, nag, or lecture others about the dangers of smoking. Focus on the benefits derived from quitting, such as better health, less coughing in the morning, more money, fewer hassles from nonsmokers, and so forth.

2) There's a fine line between nagging and encouragement. That line, of course, will vary with the individual and your relationship with the smoker. It can help to consistently (and frequently) say things like: "I care about you," "I know about the health effects of smoking and I don't want them to happen to you," and "When you're ready, I'll be there to support you." Most smokers will not consider this to be irritating nagging.

3) Remember how the addictive nature of smoking controls thinking and behavior. Most smokers continue to smoke not because they don't care about themselves or their loved ones, but because they're hooked on nicotine, lack confidence in their ability to quit, and feel that what's involved in quitting is too great a price to pay.

4) Tailor your efforts to where the smoker is in the quitting process. For those in the *precontemplation stage* (not even thinking of quitting), gently introduce the possibility of quitting and the benefits to be derived from taking that first step. For example, mention an article on the benefits of quitting that just appeared in the newspaper, or relate how others report feeling good after they quit.

For those in the *contemplation stage* (actively thinking about quitting), encourage them to take some action toward quitting, such as sending for a brochure about a quitting program, talking to their doctor about quitting, or calling a telephone quitline for assistance.

For those in the *preparation stage* (planning to take action in the near future), praise their efforts so far, express your confidence in their ability to quit, and assure them that you will help in any way you can, once they actually quit.

For those in the *action stage* (actually in the process of quitting), let them know that you're proud of the effort they're making. To reassure them, tell them that you've heard that the quitting process will get easier as time goes on, and make positive suggestions when they seem to be having a hard time. ("Let's go to the movies and get away from this for a while.")

And for those who may have *relapsed* and gone back to smoking, be positive. Never be judgmental! Tell them you know that slips do happen and that they need to learn from these experiences and become even better at saying no the next time they try to quit. Encourage them to get back on track as fast as possible, since the more quickly they stop smoking, the easier the process of staying smoke-free is likely to be. Most of all, be positive and praise the efforts they made, and never blame them for being weak or lacking willpower. Remember: Most successful quitters make several attempts before they actually get it right. Be patient and optimistic that the next attempt will work.

Finally, for those in the *maintenance phase* (people who have quit and are successfully sustaining their new smoke-free life), repeatedly tell them how proud you are of their major accomplishment and how pleased you are when you hear that they've successfully fought off their urges to smoke. In other words, reward their efforts whenever it's possible and appropriate. After the first few days of quitting, it's rare for people to get much notice or praise for their hard work. Make sure that you do recognize and reward their continuing efforts. Staying away from tobacco can be a long struggle for some people, and they need to know that others who care about them are aware of and proud of their continuing efforts. Don't be afraid to tell them so!

How to deal with the quitting smoker

Sue was only in her late 20s, but her doctor ordered her in the strongest manner possible to quit smoking because she had scleroderma, a disease that made her exceptionally vulnerable to the dangerous effects of smoking. Scleroderma patients run the risk of pulmonary fibrosis (lung scarring) and the threat of worsening circulation problems, which could lead to limb amputations. They're even cautioned against inhaling smoke from fireplaces and barbecues.

Her husband, Ed, who was generally quite supportive, told her in no uncertain terms that she *must* quit smoking and must do it immediately. While Sue agreed with him, she expressed major doubts about her ability to quit and stay the course. She told him she liked smoking and felt that it helped her control her emotions. But at the request of her physician and the urging of her husband, she agreed that she must quit. Her doctor prescribed the nicotine patch to help reduce her withdrawal symptoms.

Sue quit on a Friday and began using a patch to help control her cravings. But three days later, Ed reported that he'd just gone through the most difficult weekend of his life! Within two hours of Sue's quitting, her behavior and mood underwent incredible changes. Normally a pleasant, mild-mannered person, she became angry, hostile, demanding, and at times physically threatening to her husband.

Ed could do nothing to calm her down. He took her out to a fine restaurant, but nothing on the menu pleased her. He suggested they go to a movie, but she wanted no part of that. He even went shopping with her, something he never enjoyed doing, but she was angry and loud in the stores, which embarrassed him greatly. He tried to be understanding and patient, but nothing seemed to work. Whatever he tried to do to help her only seemed to enrage her more.

What could he do?

During the latter portions of what he later termed "my weekend in hell," he actually considered suggesting that she go back to smoking. "I couldn't stand seeing her suffer that way, and I was getting tired of how I was feeling as well," he said. "I knew she had to quit, but no one should have to go through what she was going through."

Was Sue experiencing an unusually brutal withdrawal reaction? Not exactly.

Speaking when Ed wasn't present, Sue revealed some important information. She deeply loved her husband and knew that he loved her, but she was quite angry with him for his insistence that she immediately stop smoking. When she started to feel some cravings for a cigarette, she said, "I thought of Ed telling me to quit and I just saw red!" She continued to feel that way throughout the weekend. Further questioning revealed that some of her behavior might have been designed – *unintentionally*, of course – to make him "pay" for his insistence that she quit. Finally, she revealed, "Deep down, maybe I was hoping that he'd just say 'The hell with it' and go buy me some cigarettes, so I could become my old self again." And, in fact, Ed did come very close to doing just that. Fortunately, he didn't buy her a pack, and she was eventually able to quit tobacco for good.

When a smoker quits and is going through withdrawal, be prepared for irritability, diminished frustration tolerance, and other changes in mood and behavior. Indeed, our society expects the quitting smoker to exhibit such changes, and sometimes our expectation of these changes may be a factor in triggering these emotional behaviors!

Be tolerant of these changes if they do occur. Under *no* circumstances, however, should you suggest that a person go back to smoking, no matter how cranky, depressed, or discouraged the individual may seem. Instead, suggest ways of helping the ex-smoker get through the difficult times. If you had encouraged the smoker to quit, be prepared for some anger and frustration to be directed toward you, even though your motives in urging the person to quit were the very best.

Remember: Nicotine hooks people at a brain level below the rational, thinking level. Although the quitting smoker may not consciously blame you for his or her discomfort, at some level there's likely to be a feeling that in some way you are responsible for this distress – that you "took away" the cigarettes. Be prepared for this and don't respond to the negative emotions; instead, counter with understanding words such as "I know what you're going through is hard, and I'm so proud of you!"

Ed actually followed most of these approaches correctly, even though he felt that he was coping poorly with Sue's distress.

Finally, and most important, do not "check up" on the nonsmoker by inspecting auto ashtrays, sniffing clothes for cigarette odor, or looking for cigarette butts in the trash. You cannot and must not become the "smoking police" – the force standing between a quitting smoker and his or her possible return to smoking. It is always the smoker's responsibility to quit and stay quit, not yours. Even if you do suspect that the smoking has resumed or that some cheating is going on, continue to provide praise and encouragement. Never be judgmental or pessimistic. Optimism and praise are always appropriate. Negative judgments and ridicule will not work.

In the final analysis, it's the smoker's responsibility to quit and stay quit. But important people in the smoker's life can play a very positive and important role by offering understanding, support, and patience. Quitting smoking is not an easy journey, although it turns out to be a wonderfully rewarding one. And as with any challenging passage, having friends along to share the difficulties and the triumphs can be priceless.

Chapter 10

Special Issues on the Journey to a Smoke-Free Life

It's impossible to predict what unanticipated stumbling blocks you may encounter on the road to a smoke-free life, since each person's quitting experience is unique. But hearing the stories of other quitters can give us a good idea of what kinds of issues are likely to emerge. Let's talk about some of them.

First, let's deal with the most pressing concern on most smokers' minds when they're in the quitting process: possible weight gain.

Quitting smoking and weight gain

Most smokers do gain some weight after they quit smoking, but they don't gain a lot. A recent Surgeon General's report that reviewed fifteen studies involving a total of 20,000 people found that a year after quitting, the average person's weight gain was only about five pounds. And one-fifth of the smokers gained no weight at all or actually lost weight! Less than 4 percent of those who quit gained as much as 20 pounds.

Another recent study reported that weight gain tends to peak between two and four years after quitting and then declines to the same rate as for those who never smoked.

So while horror stories abound about the incredible amounts of weight gained by people after they quit smoking, the actual facts paint a much brighter picture. And even if the worst horror story actually came true and a person gained many pounds after quitting, in all likelihood this individual would still be substantially healthier after giving up cigarettes. But of course cosmetic issues are involved here, so potential weight gain can become a serious concern for many who are quitting or anticipating quitting.

People who quit smoking may gain weight for several reasons. The most evident reason is a tendency to try to substitute one type of hunger (such as for food) for the craving for nicotine. So people attempt to smother their urge for nicotine by putting something else in their mouths – like a snack. They turn to food for emotional comfort in an effort to ease the discomfort of withdrawal.

Another reason for weight gain has to do with the role nicotine may play as an appetite suppressant. It's a sad fact that many fashion models smoke *only* because smoking decreases their urge to eat. Due to nicotine's complex effects on the release of insulin, the smoker may actually feel less hungry. This is because nicotine inhibits the release of insulin, which removes sugar from a person's blood. The smoker then becomes slightly hyperglycemic (there is more sugar in their blood than usual), and high blood sugar acts as an appetite suppressant.

Finally, quitting smoking can cause weight gain because the body begins to work more efficiently. In other words, your metabolism returns to the level it would have been at if you had never smoked at all. When you quit smoking, your body becomes more efficient in many, many ways – similar to how an automobile becomes more efficient when a hopelessly clogged air filter is replaced with a new one and the engine is once again able to get its proper supply of clean air. Unlike our attitudes toward refueling our cars (the less fuel needed, the better), most people enjoy the process of refueling themselves. So when people quit smoking, they actually need less fuel (food), but the eating habits they established as smokers were based upon much poorer fuel economy.

Thus, a combination emerges of factors that can lead to weight gain. But there are ways of combating all of them, and one of the best methods is for ex-smokers (and anyone else prone to weight gain) to weigh themselves regularly – not just after their clothes no longer fit properly! See Table 3 for more helpful suggestions.

Table 3

Principles of Weight Control After Quitting Smoking

1. Realize that weight gain can be a problem.

2. Avoid substituting food for cigarettes.

3. Use approved substitutes.

4. Avoid sugar-based products.

5. Develop a new signal to end meals.

6. Develop responses to emotions that are competitive with eating.

7. Develop or increase an exercise program.

Perhaps the most important principle is not to substitute food for cigarettes. Urges to smoke can be dealt with in many ways besides eating. It's important for you to develop coping strategies (see Chapter 8) for dealing with these urges. Go for a walk, take a shower, exercise, drink a glass of water. These activities may all help you resist the temptation to raid the cupboard or the refrigerator.

Using approved substitutes in place of high-calorie foods may also help. Water, sugarless gum and candies, celery, carrots, sunflower seeds in the shell, herbal teas (with nonsugar sweeteners), apples, and other similar high-bulk, low-calorie treats can help you avoid eating excessive amounts of food after you've quit smoking.

It's especially important to avoid sugar-based products. Several studies have shown that when people quit smoking, they're likely to crave sweets. While no harm is done to most people who eat small amounts of these treats, foods high in sugar content can become quite habit-forming. For example, if you have a chocolate bar each time you think of a cigarette, it won't take long for you to consume thousands of extra (and unnecessary) calories. It also won't take long for candy bars to become a regular staple in your life, since linkages are formed not just with cigarettes, but with food as well. For most people, taking in about 3,600 calories more than are burned through exercise or life activities leads to a one-pound weight gain. So it's critically important not to make high-calorie foods a regular substitute for cigarettes.

When most smokers end a meal, they frequently light up a cigarette. Over time, having a cigarette gradually becomes a signal to the smoker's body that the meal is over. But when a person quits smoking, there's no longer a signal that the meal is over. This frequently results in considerable difficulty ending the meal – the ex-smoker just cannot seem to finish eating, wanting one more thing, then another, and another. Obviously, if this persists for any long period, there's going to be some weight gain.

Such a person needs to develop a new signaling system that will let the body know when the meal is over. For some people, simply leaving the table promptly when they finish eating is a sufficient signal. Others may need to develop a behavior to replace the lost signal. Having a glass of water or chewing a stick of sugarless gum may, over time, develop the same signaling power that a cigarette previously held for telling the ex-smoker's body that the meal is indeed over.

Some people eat excessively in response to the emotions they're experiencing. Many eat in response to nervousness or tension. When they were smokers, they may well have turned to cigarettes when they felt these emotions. Now that they're no longer smoking, they may feel like eating something when these emotions manifest themselves. People need to develop some new responses that are competitive with these feelings. Relaxation exercises, meditation, or physical exercise can help people cope with these (and other) emotions as effectively as smoking ever did – and much more healthfully.

Finally, and perhaps most important, people who once smoked need to develop and maintain a regular exercise program. Just as our bodies were not designed to inhale poisonous smoke, they were not made for sedentary, inactive lives. Many smokers find exercise much harder than it really is, since their bodies contain multiple poisons from smoke and do not properly receive sufficient oxygen. Their muscles ache prematurely and they have a terrible time catching their breath. As a consequence, they are likely to exercise less than they should.

When people quit smoking, exercise becomes much easier. Also, it's a superb way to burn off any extra calories that may have been consumed. And exercise can have an additional benefit: It raises the metabolism (the rate at which we convert food into energy). Since this increase in metabolism often is sustained for several hours after exercise is completed, the benefit of exercise goes well beyond the immediate calories burned.

Exercise has additional benefits for ex-smokers. Regular aerobic exercise (exercise that uses large muscle groups and places demands on the cardiovascular system, such as jogging, brisk walking, and bicycling) becomes progressively easier after people quit smoking. In fact, many ex-smokers report that they are in much better physical shape than they were years and even decades earlier when they were smoking. This increase in physical stamina and vigor can be a powerful incentive to remain smoke-free forever.

Exercise can also have a very positive effect on any mood changes that may follow quitting. (We will deal with this topic more fully later in this chapter.)

In short, while many fear gaining excessive amounts of weight after they quit smoking, the truth is that most people do not experience this. Weight gain – whether feared or actual – should never, ever be used as a reason to return to smoking. There are many healthy methods for preventing weight gain and losing weight if some additional poundage does show itself after smoking has stopped. Inhaling toxic smoke that shortens life by years or even decades is not one of them!

Quitting smoking and depression

The vast majority of people who quit smoking do *not* become depressed. As discussed in Chapter 6, immediately after quitting some individuals experience withdrawal symptoms such as increased irritability, diminished frustration tolerance, anxiety, difficulty concentrating, and labile (easily changing, unstable) mood. These mood changes typically peak in one to three days and are pretty much history after about two weeks. But for a few people, more serious and longer-lasting feelings of depression can occur after they quit smoking.

What is the basis for this?

Many smokers experience a feeling of loss after they quit. Although in the long run they're going to gain tremendous physical and psychological benefits from becoming smoke-free, they feel as if they're losing something pleasurable, even essential, in their lives. Since a sense of loss can trigger feelings of gloom, it isn't surprising that many people feel depressed for a short period after they quit. It must be pointed out, however, that many people quitting smoking feel quite emotionally "up" from their first smoke-free day, since they know they're doing something very important for themselves – and they're proud!

Some people are more at risk for depression than others. People who are especially prone to depression face about a 25 percent chance of becoming depressed when they quit smoking, and this increased risk persists for at least six months following quitting. Since sad (or anxious) people may have turned to nicotine as a way to regulate negative moods, at least some of them may have used cigarettes in an attempt to "self-medicate" their depression. It's not surprising that when these people quit smoking, their depression deepens.

Here's how to deal with depression if it occurs: You need to keep reminding yourself of the wonderful gift you're giving yourself and the superb benefits you're gaining by quitting. For example, the risk of lung and other cancers and heart disease will decrease. Your blood pressure is likely to be lowered. Your immune system will become stronger. Your lung capacity will increase. You'll have more physical strength, energy, and stamina. Foods will begin to smell and taste better. And your self-esteem is likely to improve. The list goes on and on!

Positive statements to yourself can be quite beneficial, but they're not always enough. If you were diagnosed and treated for depression before you stopped smoking, you should look for any changes in symptoms. You may experience increases in depressive symptoms. If drastic mood changes occur after you quit smoking, or if they persist for an extended period, it may be time to consult a mental-health professional. A variety of treatments may be beneficial, including nicotine replacement, psychological counseling, bupropion (Zyban), or other medications.

Regular exercise can also be quite effective in combating depression. Recent studies that compared exercise and antidepressants found that regular aerobic exercise is about as effective as antidepressant medication in combating major depression for many people and may be more effective in producing lasting results. And the side effects of exercise are nearly all positive – better sleep, better sex life, and improved mental functioning. Regular exercise also benefits the heart, muscles, bones, and even the brain. New evidence suggests that being aerobically fit (having a healthy heart and lungs) may also reduce the mental decline that can occur in older adults.

There's one overriding principle here that you must never lose sight of: *No matter how depressed you or someone you care about may feel after quitting, these feelings are not a valid reason to go back to smoking.* Keep focused on the basic fact that quitting smoking is a crucial fight for survival. The fight may be hard at times, but it's worth the effort. Bad times may make it harder for you to see this, but bad times will pass. Smoking never cured anyone's depression.

If smoking comes back into your life, there's a strong likelihood that eventual health changes will make you feel even *more* depressed. Conversely, quitting smoking and living a smoke-free life are likely to be a source of pride and increased self-esteem, making depression less likely to occur down the road.

Other forms of tobacco: Cigars, pipes, and spit tobacco

Some smokers, in a very misguided effort to minimize the devastating health effects of cigarette smoking, turn to other forms of nicotine delivery such as cigars, pipes, and smokeless tobacco. Are they fooling themselves about reducing the dangerous consequences of cigarette smoking?

In a word: Yes!

Cigars and pipes expose smokers to virtually the same poisonous chemicals that cigarettes do. And smoking cigars and pipes can be as highly addictive as smoking cigarettes. If cigars and pipes are inhaled, the smoke is even more toxic than cigarette smoke. Cigar-smoking causes cancers of the lung, oral cavity (lip, tongue, mouth, throat), larynx (voice box), and esophagus, and probably cancers of the bladder and pancreas. The risk of death from lung cancer is not as high for cigar users as it is for cigarette smokers, but it is still several times higher than the risk for nonsmokers. Cigar smokers who inhale deeply and smoke several cigars a day are also at increased risk for heart disease and chronic lung disease.

Pipe smokers are at an increased risk of dying from cancers of the lung, throat, esophagus, and larynx. They're also at greater risk of dying of heart disease, stroke, and chronic lung disease than nonsmokers. The level of these risks seems to be about the same as for cigar smokers. Similar conclusions may be drawn about some of the newer and more unusual alternatives to cigarettes such as clove cigarettes, bidis (unfiltered Indian cigarettes), and hookahs. Many of these products are marketed specifically toward young people with an implication that using them is safer than smoking cigarettes. Any benefits from smoking these products might be compared to the relative benefits of being struck by an automobile at 50 miles per hour versus being struck by a truck going the same speed.

One of the fastest-growing segments of the tobacco market, especially among young people, is spit or smokeless tobacco. Smokeless tobacco enables the user to take in nicotine without actually smoking. Smokeless tobacco is available in two forms: snuff and chewing tobacco. Snuff is finely ground tobacco originally meant for sniffing. Users do not chew snuff, but put small amounts between their cheek and gum, and allow the nicotine to be absorbed into the bloodstream. It often comes in teabag-like pouches, which users "pinch" or "dip" between their lower lip and gum. Chewing tobacco – one of the oldest nicotine-delivery systems – comes in loose-leaf, plug, and twist forms. The user places a wad of it inside the cheek and chews it to mix it with saliva. The tobacco can be kept in the mouth for hours, providing an uninterrupted nicotine buzz. People become just as addicted to smokeless tobacco as they do to smoking tobacco. Some believe that spit tobacco can improve athletic performance, but no scientific evidence supports this.

There are many negative health effects of spit tobacco. In addition to permanent gum recession, chewing tobacco causes cancers of the mouth and throat as well as cardiovascular diseases. Devastating health effects can occur quite quickly; cancers have been found in the mouths of those who have used the product regularly for only six years. The Centers for Disease Control reports that snuff users are fifty times more likely than nonusers to develop certain cancers of the gum or the lining of the inner cheek and are four times more likely to get cancer of the mouth.

In addition to the health effects, smokeless tobacco produces such socially undesirable effects as spitting, drooling, bad breath, and stained teeth.

Throughout this book, primary emphasis has been on cigarettes and ways of quitting smoking. Well, virtually everything that has been said about cigarette smoking applies to pipes and cigars as well. Most pipe and cigar smokers have somewhat fewer linkages to break since they don't typically smoke as much or in as many settings as cigarette smokers. But otherwise, there are few differences between quitting cigarettes and ending pipe and cigar use.

In many ways, ending spit tobacco use is much like ending the addiction to cigarettes, pipes, or cigars – the same mental and behavioral preparation is necessary, and similar quitting techniques are used, including nicotine-replacement therapy. But there are a couple of differences worth noting. With spit tobacco, there's often a stronger need for some type of oral substitute (such as gum) to take the place of the chewing or sniffing. Also, the disappearance of mouth and gum sores soon after quitting provides a readily visible – and remarkably powerful – benefit of quitting.

Chapter 11

Social and Political Issues

The primary focus of this book has been to explore tobacco use and how stopping smoking can lead to a healthier and happier life. But now it's time to turn to the historical, political, and social forces that went into creating a product that prematurely kills more than 400,000 Americans each year and makes countless others ill and old before their time.

Knowledge of these factors may not provide the necessary stimulus for smokers to quit. Yet awareness of how the tobacco industry has amassed its power and sought to influence society is absolutely necessary if we want to successfully change people's minds and prevent millions more of our citizens from becoming addicted – and poisoned – by tobacco products.

Most people would agree that one of the most fundamental functions of government is to provide security for its citizens. That security includes protecting its people from invading armies, but it goes beyond that. Guarding the public's health is another fundamental duty of government. National, state, and local authorities go to great lengths to ensure that our water supply is protected, that our food isn't contaminated by poisons, that our roads are safe to drive, and that our air is safe to breathe. But when it comes to safeguarding people from the ravages of tobacco, our elected officials – with but a few exceptions – have failed miserably to protect us. They have consistently looked the other way while a multibillion-dollar industry has grown increasingly richer and the users of its products have become ill and died by the millions.

Why has this happened, and why is there not a greater outcry from the public? Let's start at the beginning.

A brief history of tobacco

Tobacco was unknown to the western world until the time of Columbus, although it was used in the Americas by native peoples for more than 5,000 years. Just as Columbus is credited by many with "discovering" America,

he's also credited with "discovering" tobacco. In the century after Columbus, tobacco use spread so quickly throughout Europe that the 17th century has come to be described as the "great age of the pipe." During the 18th century, snuff was the preferred means of using tobacco; one hundred years later, the cigar was king. Tobacco also came to be used as a monetary standard – literally, it was a cash crop throughout the 18th century and lasted twice as long as the gold standard.

Thousands of people merrily puffed away, oblivious to the effects of tobacco on the human body. Then, in 1761, an English physician named John Hill made the first clinical study of tobacco's effects and issued a warning to snuff users that they were vulnerable to cancers of the nose.

Gradually, more and more information began to accumulate about tobacco's negative effects on health. But because tobacco was an immensely profitable product, within the governments of most countries this information fell on deaf ears. With users quickly becoming addicted to the nicotine in tobacco, it became a lucrative (and steadily increasing) source of income not just for the farmers and industries that produced it, but also for the governments that taxed it. For example, British tobacco taxes were a major factor along the "Tobacco Coast" (Chesapeake Bay), where the Revolutionary War was labeled "the Tobacco War."

After James Bonsack invented the cigarette-making machine in 1881, cigarette smoking became widespread. Bonsack's cigarette machine could make 120,000 cigarettes a day, an output that revolutionized the tobacco industry. He went into business with James "Buck" Duke and built a factory that made 10 million cigarettes the first year and about 1 billion cigarettes five years later. Cigarettes quickly became the nicotine-delivery system of choice. They were cheap to produce, easy to use, and enormously profitable.

Cigarettes were smoked primarily by men – it was not considered "proper" for women to smoke. The first brand of cigarettes was called "Duke of Durham" and packaged in a box with baseball cards. Even back then, the tobacco industry recognized the importance of recruiting young people for its deadly products.

World Wars I and II were good for the tobacco industry. In both wars, American soldiers overseas were given free cigarettes every day, and millions of GIs quickly became hooked. By 1944, cigarette production was up to 300 billion a year, and servicemen received about 75 percent of all cigarettes produced.

During World War II, cigarettes began to be heavily marketed directly to women. The war brought independence for many women – collectively symbolized by Rosie the Riveter – who went to work and started smoking while their husbands were away. Ironically, as the war helped "emancipate" women, tobacco enslaved them through its powerful addictive properties.

Before World War II, cases of lung cancer were extremely rare among women. By 1986, roughly four decades after the war ended, lung cancer had surpassed breast cancer as the number one cause of cancer deaths among women. About 85 percent of all lung cancer is caused by tobacco use. And, of course, smoking kills thousands of additional women each year through heart and other circulatory diseases, emphysema, and other forms of cancer.

At the same time as tobacco use was dramatically growing, evidence of its devastating effects on the human body was gradually accumulating. In the early years of the 20th century, tobacco manufacturers apparently weren't completely aware of the dangers of their product. But by the 1940s, the scientific case against cigarettes was mounting; it became widely known to the public by the 1950s, a time when more than half the American population smoked and cigarettes were an accepted part of life. In 1964, "Smoking and Health: Report of the Advisory Committee to the Surgeon

General," the first major U.S. report on smoking and health, was published. This landmark Surgeon General's Report summarized a great deal of scientific evidence and concluded that cigarette smoking was a cause of lung cancer. For the first time in history, the U.S. government had officially declared tobacco a major health hazard.

How did the tobacco industry respond to the accumulating and eventually overwhelming evidence that its products were damaging the health of the nation? Did its leaders immediately begin searching for a means to make their product less dangerous, as the automobile industry, for example, has consistently done when hazards were found in its cars?

Of course not. The tobacco companies denied that their products posed a health danger. And they used an arsenal of tactics to divert the public's attention from the issue. They hired their own "experts," who attempted to cast doubt upon the validity of the research and created a "debate" over whether smoking was really harmful – when no debate whatsoever existed among reputable scientists.

In the early 1950s, the link between smoking and lung cancer, which had been discussed and confirmed in medical journals, began to attract the attention of the media. The tobacco companies publicly denied that smoking was dangerous, asserting that the only acceptable scientific "proof" to demonstrate that smoking was harmful would be a classic experimental design study. In such a study, they argued, children would be randomly assigned at birth to "smoking" and "nonsmoking" groups and then followed for a lifetime to see whether the smoking groups were significantly less healthy (and died younger) than the nonsmoking groups. In addition to the impossibility of carrying out a study like this, to perform such research would be blatantly unethical!

In other words, the tobacco industry denied the value of standard, scientifically accepted epidemiological research that had been used for decades to demonstrate relationships between environmental influences and many types of illnesses. Even though research was clearly demonstrating how dangerous tobacco products were, the tobacco industry claimed that the case had not been proven.

The tobacco companies also hired high-powered public-relations firms to cast their products in a favorable light. They spent billions of dollars to advertise and promote their products in the media, with a good deal of this directed toward recruiting youth. They donated millions of dollars each year to lawmakers at all levels of government to prevent meaningful regulation of tobacco products. In short, they used a clever and cynical approach to continue to make billions of dollars selling a product that their own documents revealed was by far the most dangerous ever made, all the while claiming that tobacco was a "legal product" and therefore the government had no right to regulate it – even though all types of legal products from automobiles to toasters to baby cribs are regulated by government.

Although it publicly denied that the dangers of smoking had been proven, the tobacco industry, threatened with the loss of jittery customers, went on the offensive in the 1950s and introduced "safer" cigarettes – cigarettes with filters. To accompany these new brands, the tobacco industry unleashed a marketing blitz to reassure smokers that their health was not in jeopardy. One of the first of these new filter cigarettes was L&M Filters, which were advertised as "just what the doctor ordered!" while Parliaments claimed to provide "maximum health protection."

R$_x$

"Just what the doctor ordered."

Kent cigarettes, with their "Micronite" filters, made the biggest splash of all. Kent was promoted as the brand for "the 1 out of every 3 smokers who is unusually sensitive to tobacco tars and nicotine." But what did Kent's cigarette filters really contain? According to the manufacturer, as stated in its ads, "a pure, dust-free, completely harmless material that is so safe, so effective, it actually is used to help filter the air in hospital operating rooms." In reality, the Micronite filter – whose actual composition the ads never revealed – *contained a par-*

ticularly dangerous form of asbestos. There was asbestos in the Micronite filter from 1952 until about 1957. During this time, according to sales figures, Americans puffed their way through more than 13 billion Kent cigarettes, asbestos and all. It was well known at that time in the scientific community that asbestos caused lung cancer. Yet Kent cigarettes with Micronite asbestos filters were cynically – and deceptively – marketed as "the greatest health protection in cigarette history."

It is unknown whether Kent smokers inhaled asbestos from the filter and whether they experienced a higher rate of cancer than smokers of other brands – statistics on this have never been revealed. But what is well documented is the very high death rate of workers who manufactured these asbestos-filled filters. Many died of asbestosis, lung cancer, or mesothelioma, an extremely rare and virulent form of cancer almost invariably caused by asbestos inhalation.

Kent cigarette manufacturers quietly took the asbestos out of its Micronite filters without ever admitting that those filters had actually contained asbestos. And no government agency or congressional watchdog committee ever looked into this incredible abuse of the public's health.

After marketing filter cigarettes in a manner suggesting that they might protect smokers from dangers that the tobacco companies wouldn't even admit existed, their next clever marketing ploy involved so-called "low tar and nicotine" or "light" cigarettes. Light cigarettes are so designated because they deliver less nicotine and lower levels of toxic chemicals *when the smoke is measured by a machine.* In real life, however, smokers inhale amounts of nicotine and tobacco chemicals in light cigarettes comparable to those in ordinary cigarettes. People who use light cigarettes may, for example, inhale more deeply to obtain more nicotine, or they'll simply smoke more cigarettes. In some cases, light cigarettes have minute vent holes drilled into their filters, holes that smokers may (with or without awareness) cover up while smoking in order to get a more "satisfying" taste – receiving, of course, much more tar and nicotine than is measured by the machines, which did not cover up these holes.

Numerous studies have found these so-called light cigarettes to be just as deadly as regular ones even though a substantial proportion of smokers believe that it's safer to smoke these cigarettes. Since their introduction in the United States in the late 1960s, light cigarettes have grown to account for roughly 85 percent of cigarette sales.

But is it easier to quit when a smoker is smoking lights? Not at all. A 2006 study of more than 12,000 smokers by Dr. Hilary Tindle and her colleagues found that those who used light cigarettes were about 50 percent less likely to quit smoking than those who smoked non-light cigarettes. As with filter cigarettes, the marketing of light cigarettes was a tobacco-industry ploy that ended up doing substantial damage to people who thought they were reducing the health risks of smoking.

How does the tobacco industry get by with putting asbestos into its filters or suggesting that its light cigarettes are less dangerous when they are really more dangerous? Shouldn't the government be protecting people from these misleading and eventually deadly marketing ploys?

Government's role in protecting the public

A fundamental, profound, and very disquieting truth emerges regarding the relationship between our government and the tobacco industry. Although an assortment of efforts have been made by the federal government over the years to warn the public of the dangers of tobacco use, few successful attempts have ever been made to *control and reduce the dangers*

SURGEON GENERAL'S WARNING:
Smoking Causes Lung Cancer
Heart Disease, Emphysema, And
May Complicate Pregnancy

tobacco inflicts upon the public. Tobacco, which kills more citizens each year than auto accidents, homicides, suicides, and illegal drugs put together, is not regulated by any federal agency. It's the only consumer product entering the human body that is completely unregulated (except for the taxes it generates for governments at all levels). The Food and Drug Administration can regulate a bag of potato chips or a tube of lipstick but not a pack of cigarettes.

The tobacco industry has long taken advantage of this lack of regulation to market its deadly products to children, deceive consumers about the harm its products cause, and resist any meaningful effort to make its products less harmful or less addictive. For example, if a tobacco manufacturer were to increase the amount of arsenic in its cigarettes by, say, 100 times, no agency would have to be notified, since no agency is currently empowered to monitor tobacco products. Indeed, the manufacturers of filter cigarettes could reintroduce asbestos (or any other cancer-causing compound) into their products without worrying about any regulatory action – except, perhaps, for the court of public opinion, if it became known that asbestos was back in filter cigarettes!

As mentioned earlier, the Surgeon General issued a landmark report in 1964 about the dangers of cigarette smoking. This report clearly documented the causal relationship between smoking cigarettes and lung cancer. In 1965, Congress passed the Cigarette Labeling and Advertising Act, which stated that every cigarette pack must have a warning label on its side stating, "Cigarettes may be hazardous to your health." These laws required a health warning on cigarette packages, banned cigarette advertising in the broadcasting media, and called for an annual report on the health consequences of smoking. These historic actions of Congress were the first major steps ever taken by that legislative body to deal with the problems caused by tobacco. Unfortunately, in the more than forty years since, Congress has not passed any significant legislation that matched those initial efforts in tobacco control – which were, of course, basically warnings and not meaningful tobacco *control* measures. Meanwhile, the tobacco industry, which initially opposed the warnings, has cleverly used them to argue in lawsuits against it that the population has been advised of tobacco's dangers and should know better than to use its dangerous products – and, therefore, the industry that manufactures them should assume no liability for the vast number of deaths and illnesses they cause!

Why are there no federal regulations (except for taxes collected) on tobacco products? The answer is simple: *money!* Tobacco is enormously profitable for the manufacturers who produce it and the governments that tax it. In addition, cigarette taxes help pay for sports stadiums and fund arts and community programs around the country.

In order to protect its lucrative profits, the tobacco industry spends millions of dollars each year on lobbying and campaign contributions. This industry is one of the biggest spenders in Congress and many state legislatures. For example, during the 2003-2004 election cycle, the tobacco industry gave more than $2 million in contributions directly to *federal* candidates alone. And many of our lawmakers at the national and state levels consistently vote to protect the profits of the tobacco industry while seemingly ignoring how its products adversely affect the health of constituents. Elected to protect the welfare of their constituents, they end up protecting the profits of the tobacco industry and in the process sell out the health of the public, all the while proclaiming that tobacco is, after all, a legal product.

But it's not only the money the tobacco industry contributes to lawmakers that influences the lack of meaningful regulation of tobacco products. Federal and state taxes collected on tobacco products are an important source of revenue for national and state governments. In 2003 (the most recent year for which data were available) the federal government collected about $8 billion dollars in tobacco tax revenues. The fifty states collectively taxed tobacco products more than $11 billion that year – not including the sales taxes also charged on tobacco products. In short, governments at all levels depend upon tobacco as an important source of revenue. However, this view is extremely shortsighted. For example, the U.S. General Accounting Office in 2002 estimated that $76 billion in medical expenditures and $92 billion in lost productivity were attributable to cigarette smoking. If tobacco products indeed were to pay for all the damage they inflict on society, the taxes on them would be astronomical.

One additional factor complicating this picture is the role taxes play in deterring smoking. Increases in cigarette prices lead to significant reductions in cigarette smoking. A 10 percent increase in price has been estimated by the Centers for Disease Control to reduce overall cigarette consumption by about 3 to 5 percent. Increases in cigarette prices especially lead to significant reductions in smoking among young smokers. Every 10 percent increase in the price of cigarettes cuts youth smoking by about 7 percent. Indeed, a 2000 Surgeon General's report concluded that "raising tobacco taxes is one of the most effective tobacco control and prevention tactics." So our governments raise taxes on tobacco – a good thing in terms of reducing tobacco use and one of the few actual tobacco control measures passed by Congress – and in the process, these governments become even more dependent upon this source of income to finance their operations!

Meanwhile, the government continues to warn of the dangers of tobacco use. "Reducing Tobacco Use," a 2000 Surgeon General's report, calls tobacco use the "number one cause of preventable disease and death" in the United States. According to Dr. David Satcher, the Surgeon General at that time, "Tobacco use will remain the leading cause of preventable illness and death in this nation and a growing number of other countries until tobacco prevention and control efforts are commensurate with the harm caused by tobacco use."

In all, thirty reports have been issued by the Surgeon General since 1964 documenting in great detail the dangerous consequences of smoking and warning the public against its use. But only recently have there been some attempts to protect the public from the proven ravages of smoking.

In 1996, the FDA asserted jurisdiction over tobacco products under the Food, Drug, and Cosmetic Act with regulations designed to regulate tobacco advertising, promotional campaigns, and labeling and purchasing restrictions. The tobacco industry sued the federal government, arguing that the FDA lacked legal authority to regulate its products. The United States Supreme Court ruled in June 2000 that Congress had not expressly given the FDA legal authority to regulate the tobacco industry and that Congress must specifically enact legislation to allow the FDA to regulate tobacco. As a result, all FDA tobacco regulations were dropped, including the federal minimum-age requirement for tobacco products (18 years old), as well as federal rules requiring retailers to check photo identification. Once again, the tobacco industry had successfully defeated attempts to regulate its products and protect the public.

Since then, there have been attempts in Congress to authorize the FDA to regulate tobacco products. At the time of this writing, these efforts have been unsuccessful, in large part due to the lobbying of the tobacco industry. Legislation is pending in Congress that would empower the FDA to oversee – and potentially, modify for the public's welfare – many aspects of the manufacturing, marketing, labeling, distribution, and sale of tobacco products. These measures could significantly reduce the number of people who start to smoke, substantially increase the number of smokers who quit, and reduce harm to those who are unable to quit. As essential as this legislation is, lobbyists from the tobacco industry have been successful thus far in keeping it stalled in committee. Once again, the tobacco industry seems to be having its way at the expense of the public's health.

The historic tobacco settlement:
A blessing for the public or the tobacco industry?

If legislative and executive efforts to control tobacco products seem futile, what about turning to another branch of government, the judicial?

Over the years, a number of lawsuits were launched against the tobacco industry by individuals who insisted that they were harmed by its products. The tobacco industry – with its deep pockets and cadres of clever attorneys – managed to win virtually all of these suits. Despite these wins, however, the tobacco companies became increasingly worried that losing one or more major lawsuits would seriously reduce their enormous profits. Their worry increased when a large number of previously secret documents became public. (Now known as the "Secret Tobacco Documents," they can be read on the Internet – see Appendix 2.) These documents clearly indicated that tobacco company executives knew all about the lethal and addictive nature of tobacco, conspired to hide this information from the public, and tried to keep a "debate" going over whether tobacco was indeed harmful. For example, in 1994, seven leaders of major American tobacco companies stated under oath at a congressional hearing that nicotine was *not* addictive – yet their own secret documents revealed that they knew tobacco was addictive; hence, they were lying to Congress and the American people. This action was highly publicized and further fueled public outrage at the tobacco companies, which were feeling increasingly vulnerable.

In the 1990s, states banded together. Asserting that tobacco companies had lied about the health risks of smoking and run up state Medicaid costs in treating sick smokers over the years, they threatened a massive lawsuit against tobacco manufacturers. Eventually, the tobacco companies decided to settle the state lawsuits without going to court. The tobacco companies agreed to a deal with lawyers representing forty states. Under the terms of the settlement, the industry agreed to pay approximately $246 billion over twenty-five years for the health-care costs incurred in the treatment of people with smoking-related illnesses. In return, the deal would stop further class-action lawsuits against the tobacco industry and impose a limit on the amount of money required to pay future individual claimants.

One of the understandings from this so-called "Master Settlement" was that a substantial portion of the funds the states received from the tobacco industry would go toward helping smokers quit and preventing potential new smokers from starting – in short, toward tobacco control. Unfortunately, however, this was only an understanding, since nothing was actually written into the Master Settlement *requiring* this to be done. In fact, precious little of that money has gone toward tobacco control. States have so far spent the vast majority of the money on a wide range of programs unrelated to treating sick smokers or reducing smoking rates, according to an annual report by the General Accounting Office.

The tobacco companies, as it turned out, did quite well in the settlement. They raised cigarette prices beyond the actual settlement costs and in the process gained protection from potentially massive payouts from future lawsuits. At the end of the day, the tobacco industry received substantial protection from litigation and even greater profits than before, the states received monies for their budgets with no restrictions on how they should be spent, and the lawyers who negotiated the settlements received an estimated $13 billion in legal fees.

Several states did manage to direct some of their funds to initiate smoking-prevention and cessation programs for their citizens, programs that demonstrably reduced tobacco use for youths and adults. Unfortunately, in a number of cases in later years states that had received money for tobacco-control programs redirected those funds toward other purposes. For the most part, however, the really big winners in the Tobacco Settlement were the state government treasuries, the attorneys who negotiated the settlement, and the tobacco companies that received immunity from lawsuits. As has so often been the case historically, when the interests of the tobacco industry conflict with the health and welfare of the public, public health interests come in last.

The clean indoor air movement

Most of the smoke generated by burning tobacco and cigarette paper is released into the environment. Secondhand smoke is a mixture of the exhalation of smokers and the fumes that come from the burning end of a cigarette, cigar, or pipe. It is also referred to as environmental tobacco smoke, passive smoke, or involuntary smoke.

Hundreds of studies have clearly documented that direct smoking is extremely dangerous to the smoker. The question is whether environmental tobacco smoke (which is more diluted than direct smoke) also poses a significant danger to those who breathe it. Initially, it was felt that secondhand smoke was mostly an annoyance – irritating to many who were forced to breathe it but not really dangerous. But as more and more research accumulated, it gradually became apparent that environmental smoke was considerably *more* than an irritation to those who breathed it.

In early 1993, the Environmental Protection Agency released a report that evaluated the respiratory health effects from breathing secondhand smoke. In that report, the EPA concluded that secondhand smoke causes lung cancer in adult nonsmokers and impairs the respiratory health of children. These findings were very similar to ones made previously by the National Academy of Sciences and the Surgeon General. The EPA report classified secondhand smoke as a Group A carcinogen, a designation which means that there is sufficient evidence that the substance causes cancer in humans. The Group A designation has been used by the EPA for only fifteen other pollutants, including asbestos, radon, and benzene. But of all these Group A cancer-causing pollutants, only secondhand smoke has actually been shown in studies to cause cancer at *typical environmental levels*. In that report, the EPA estimated that about 3,000 American nonsmokers die each year from lung cancer caused by secondhand smoke.

The tobacco companies lobbied hard against these scientific findings. They employed the political process – which ultimately did not work – to suppress the information and cast major doubt upon it. Just as it had done many times in the past to dispute the health hazards of direct smoking, the tobacco industry and its paid spokesmen attempted to confuse the public about the dangers of secondhand smoke. These companies realized that reducing and eventually eliminating smoking in all public places would cut deeply into their profits, since smokers would be smoking less and some might quit altogether once they realized they could indeed go several hours without smoking.

The tobacco companies also knew that eliminating smoking in public places would be a large step toward "de-normalizing" smoking – transforming the public image of smoking that they have tried so hard to present as glamorous, sexy, and adventuresome, and repositioning it in its rightful place as an extremely unhealthy behavior that is life-threatening to both those who smoke and those unlucky enough to be exposed to the smoke from others. After all, the tobacco companies had spent (and are still spending) many billions of dollars each year on advertising and marketing, trying to generate a highly positive image of tobacco as a substance that enhances life.

In 2006, the Surgeon General released a landmark report that stifled the debate over whether secondhand smoke was dangerous. This report, titled "The Health Consequences of Involuntary Exposure to Tobacco Smoke: A Report of the Surgeon General," concluded that:

1) Secondhand smoke exposure causes disease and premature death in children and adults who do not smoke.

2) Children exposed to secondhand smoke are at an increased risk for sudden infant death syndrome, acute respiratory infections, ear problems, and severe asthma.

3) Smoking by parents causes respiratory symptoms and slows lung growth in their children.

4) Exposure of adults to secondhand smoke has immediate adverse effects on the cardiovascular system and causes coronary heart disease and lung cancer.

5) The scientific evidence indicates that there is no risk-free level of exposure to secondhand smoke. About 49,000 U.S. citizens die prematurely each year from the effects of secondhand smoke, with the vast majority of deaths caused by heart disease.

This report concluded that only by eliminating smoking in indoor spaces can nonsmokers be protected fully from exposure to secondhand smoke. Simply separating smokers from nonsmokers, cleaning the air, and ventilating buildings cannot stop nonsmokers from coming in contact with secondhand smoke.

In short, this latest Surgeon General's report summarized a wealth of evidence that environmental tobacco smoke is indeed dangerous to all who breathe it. The report, written by twenty-two national experts, was scientifically irrefutable. The report's chapters were then reviewed by forty peer reviewers, and the entire document was reviewed by thirty independent scientists and by lead scientists within the Centers for Disease Control and Prevention and the Department of Health and Human Services. Throughout the review process, the report was revised to address reviewers' comments and reflected a careful, scientific review of all the information in the world regarding the effect of secondhand smoke on those who breathe it.

There are, of course, a few who continue to dispute the report's findings and conclusions. Virtually all these individuals are either paid spokesmen for the tobacco industry and its allies, or offbeat "scientists" who have not subjected their writings and research to a peer-review process (in which other scientists in the field examine their methods, data, and conclusions). Unfortunately, a number of misguided souls continue from a variety of motivations to argue that the case against secondhand smoke is junk science that has not been proven, just as many other questionable "experts" once said that the negative health effects of direct smoking had not been established.

The general public understands the dangers of secondhand smoke. A number of public opinion surveys throughout the country have demonstrated that clear majorities – at times as high as 80 percent or more – recognize secondhand smoke as dangerous and support measures to eliminate it from all indoor public places. At the time of this writing, twenty-one states (plus the District of Columbia, Puerto Rico, and Guam) prohibit smoking in restaurants. Of these jurisdictions, seventeen prohibit indoor smoking in virtually all public places. Hundreds of communities in other states have elected to go smoke-free as well. Clearly, the momentum is shifting in favor of protecting the rights of people to breathe clean air and against the purported rights of smokers to pollute the air that others must breathe.

The future of tobacco control

Throughout this book, there has been repeated mention of the splendid rewards of moving from being a tobacco user to learning to embrace a smoke-free life. Because this book was intended primarily to help those enslaved by tobacco to become tobacco-free, little has been said of the steps our society could take to make a similarly wonderful journey.

How can we begin to end the death, misery, and financial costs caused by tobacco consumption? Since tobacco is a legal product by virtue of history (definitely not merit), there is virtually no likelihood that its use will be outlawed. Such a prohibition, if enacted, would almost certainly be doomed to failure and would most likely create massive illegal activity as tobacco users of all ages would do whatever was necessary to ensure an uninterrupted supply of their addictive products. Instead of a grand move such as outlawing tobacco, society will need to pursue a series of steps: an incremental, gradual, yet steady and unrelenting process toward becoming smoke-free.

An indispensable first step in this effort would be to subject tobacco products to the same type of regulation that is applied to virtually all products that are taken into or interact with the human body. As of this writing, legislation to enable the FDA to regulate certain aspects of tobacco products is stalled in the Congress. Currently, manufacturers of tobacco products are not required to reveal to anybody what the poisonous ingredients of their products are or how they may have been recently modified or even increased. No other consumer product enjoys such an exemption from governmental scrutiny. The fact that this exemption is granted to the product that has caused *many times more deaths than all our other consumer products put together* is deplorable. There is a desperate need for meaningful regulation of tobacco products, and we must insist that our lawmakers do the right thing.

Action is also needed to absolutely prohibit all forms of tobacco marketing to youth. Young people are, after all, the future customers for (and eventual victims of) tobacco. While the tobacco industry says it has "voluntarily" curbed some types of blatant promotion of its products to young people, it continues to work hard in more subtle ways to make its lethal products seem attractive to youth. When a deadly, addictive product kills upwards of 400,000 citizens each year and burdens society with astronomical expenses in health-care costs and lost income, does it really have a right to advertise at all? Constitutional scholars may debate this point. Do corporations enjoy the same freedom of speech as individuals, especially when they are promoting products that inflict so much damage on society?

Over the centuries, society has glamorized tobacco use. It has been made to look sexy, grown-up, exciting, adventuresome, masculine, feminine, a sign of success, and so forth. These false images have been consciously and expertly fashioned by the tobacco industry and by those who stand to benefit from its enormous profits. Just as clever advertising and marketing have created these false images, we must strive to replace them with the truth. And the truth is simple and straightforward: Tobacco is a deadly product that addicts its users, robs them of their health, sends many of them prematurely to their graves, and inflicts terrible financial and emotional costs on society.

Put another way, tobacco use is a completely aberrant behavior that should not be respected or emulated in any way. It is one of the most unattractive behaviors that people can engage in. Our youth – indeed, our entire population – needs to receive this message often and powerfully from many different sources.

Advertisements must be created that convey the complete abnormality of tobacco use in every way possible, including direct educational efforts that begin with young children.

We should also outlaw smoking in all public places, not just to protect public health but to denormalize smoking.

Cigarettes and other tobacco products must be kept out of sight in stores.

Smoking by actors in movies and television programs should be prohibited wherever it is clearly not essential to the plot. The Centers for Disease Control and Prevention named tobacco use in films as a major factor in teen smoking. Research shows that the depiction of smoking in movies is the most powerful pro-tobacco influence on kids today, an effect even stronger than cigarette advertising.

Much more needs to be done in the realm of tobacco prevention and smoking cessation. Public programs exist that are definitely effective in preventing people from starting smoking and helping tobacco users quit, but they are not universally available and they should be. What better use is there for our tax dollars than to direct them into programs that prevent illness and premature death, and at the same time reduce the enormous financial burdens placed on our society by tobacco?

In short, our society needs to do everything possible to regulate tobacco, discourage its use among all citizens, and help those who are addicted to its products to stop using them. Tobacco growers and manufacturers need to be encouraged – and even assisted, where necessary – to develop other sources of income to replace the profits from their deadly products. This overall effort requires more than a piecemeal approach whereby certain municipalities (and sometimes, states) undertake positive programs.

What is needed is a sustained, multifaceted, and powerful effort that is national in scope and whose benefits are directed toward every citizen. Then and only then – when the death and destruction caused by tobacco products are no longer tolerated by the public – will our society complete its grand journey to an existence without the blight of tobacco usage and enjoy the many benefits we can derive from a *truly* smoke-free society.

Appendix 1

DeNelsky-Plesec
Stop Smoking Checklist

The DeNelsky-Plesec Stop Smoking Checklist is a guide to quitting smoking. Developed by the author and his colleague at the Cleveland Clinic, psychologist Dr. Thomas L. Plesec, this list mirrors the type of checklist an airplane pilot might refer to before taking off and landing. People can use this checklist as a helpful resource to guide their actions as they prepare for quitting, as they maintain their quitting during the first two weeks of nonsmoking, and as they remain smoke-free after two weeks and after two months.

PREPARING TO QUIT

_____ Make a pact with yourself to quit.

_____ Pick your quitting date. (My date is _____.)

_____ Write the three most important reasons for quitting on a card, and carry that card with you everywhere you go. Look at it several times each day to remind yourself of why you want to quit.

_____ Prior to quitting, completely eliminate smoking in two or three of your high-risk situations. For example, don't smoke after a meal or when you see a traffic jam up ahead.

_____ Reduce consumption to one pack per day or less.

_____ Change to a less desirable brand of cigarettes.

_____ Discard your lighter and begin using matches. Carry your cigarettes in a different place.

_____ Spend a little time each day visualizing stressful events occurring in the future and see yourself not smoking as a reaction to those events.

QUITTING: The first two weeks

_____ Get rid of **ALL** cigarettes! Put away all smoking-related objects such as ashtrays. Ask people you live with not to smoke in your presence for two weeks.

_____ Spend as much time as possible with nonsmoking people.

_____ Keep busy, especially on evenings and weekends.

_____ Avoid high-risk situations like large parties and bars.

_____ Spend lots of time in places that prohibit smoking, like theaters and libraries.

_____ Drink plenty of fluids.

_____ Don't substitute food or sugar-based products for cigarettes. Use approved substitutes like ice water, high-bulk/low-calorie foods (apples, carrots, celery), and sugarless gum.

_____ Begin (or increase) a regular exercise program.

_____ When experiencing withdrawal effects:

1. Keep reminding yourself why you're quitting (read that card you carry with you).

2. Keep reminding yourself that whatever discomfort you're experiencing is much better than the unhealthy outcomes of continued smoking (painful diseases, surgery, chemotherapy).

3. Practice deep breathing or other relaxation techniques.

_____ Always remember that you're freeing yourself from an expensive, messy habit by becoming a nonsmoker.

MAINTENANCE OF QUITTING: After two weeks

____ Keep reminding yourself that the desire to smoke is linked to many situations, people, and emotional states.

____ Remember that your desire to smoke will last only a few seconds; distract yourself or do something different, if necessary.

____ After each craving to smoke has passed, give yourself a pat on the back – you've just made great progress in breaking your habit forever.

____ Save the money you used to waste on cigarettes in a special fund, and then buy yourself something nice.

MAINTENANCE OF QUITTING: After two months

____ Be particularly vigilant when unusual life events occur (weddings, holidays, vacation).

____ Be particularly vigilant when stressful life events occur (relationship, financial, or work-related problems).

____ Keep reminding yourself that not smoking is probably the most important gift you can give yourself.

____ Keep reminding yourself that not smoking is completely within your personal control.

____ NEVER lull yourself into thinking you're out of danger and you can safely have a cigarette or two. You can't!

____ If, by chance, you do slip and have a cigarette, don't give up! All is not lost. Return to complete abstinence immediately, and learn from your experience.

____ If you've gained significant weight since quitting, now is the time to do something about it. Start going for walks, or begin an exercise program.

____ Each time you see a cigarette advertisement, remind yourself why you quit (read your card). Also, remember that a powerful industry spends billions of dollars each year trying to get people like you "re-hooked."

Appendix 2

General Tobacco Resources

Here are some good sources of reliable information on the dangers of smoking and the process of quitting.

Action on Smoking and Health (ASH)
(Information for people concerned about smoking and nonsmokers' rights, smoking statistics, quitting smoking, smoking risks, and other news.)
2013 H Street, N.W. • Washington, D.C. 20006
(202) 659-4310
http://www.ash.org/

American Cancer Society
(The American Cancer Society's website contains considerable material about smoking and quitting.)
(800) ACS-2345
(866) 228-4327 (TTY).
http://www.cancer.org/docroot/home/index.asp

American Heart Association
(The mission of the American Heart Association is to reduce disability and death from cardiovascular diseases and stroke. The website covers smoking and cardiovascular diseases, and smoking cessation.)
7272 Greenville Avenue • Dallas, Texas 75231-4596
(214) 706-1179
http://www.americanheart.org

American Lung Association
(The American Lung Association promotes lung health, and the group's website presents news regarding tobacco use.)
61 Broadway, 6th Floor • New York, New York 10006
(800) 548-8252
(212) 315-8700 (National Headquarters)
http://www.lungusa.org

Centers for Disease Control and Prevention
(The website presents information on smoking and health, and other related topics.)
1600 Clifton Road, N.E. • Atlanta, Georgia 30333
(404) 639-3311
Public Inquiries: (404) 639-3534 / (800) 311-3435
http://www.cdc.gov/tobacco/

National Cancer Institute
(The website presents information on tobacco use and cancer.)
NCI Public Inquiries Office
6116 Executive Boulevard • Room 3036A
Bethesda, Maryland 20892-8322
(800) 4-CANCER / (1-800-422-6237)
http://www.cancer.gov/help

National Center for Chronic Disease Prevention and Health Promotion –
Tobacco Information and Prevention Source (TIPS)
(This website has all the Surgeon General's Reports on tobacco, including updates on the dangers of environmental tobacco smoke.)
http://www.cdc.gov/tobacco/sgr/index.htm

National Institute on Drug Abuse
(This arm of the National Institutes of Health, an agency of the U.S. Department of Health and Human Services, focuses on fighting drug abuse and addiction, including tobacco addiction.)
http://www.nida.nih.gov/Infofacts/Tobacco.html

Office of the Surgeon General
(The website features all of the Surgeon General's Reports.)
5600 Fishers Lane
Room 18-66
Rockville, MD 20857
(301) 443-4000
http://www.surgeongeneral.gov/contactus.html

Tobacco Documents Online

(As part of the Master Settlement Agreement between the United States and the tobacco companies, the industry was required to make all documents used during the trials available. This readily searchable website contains over 4 million documents!)

http://tobaccodocuments.org/

Tobacco Control Resource Center

(This nonprofit organization seeks to reduce the public's use of tobacco products. It provides legal research, litigation support, and policy analysis for advocates of tobacco control throughout the world.)

102 The Fenway

Cushing Hall, Suite 117

Boston, Massachusetts 02115

(617) 373-2026

http://www.tobacco.neu.edu

U.S. Department of Health and Human Services –
Tobacco Cessation Resources

(This website offers materials for professionals and consumers, including the latest information to help people quit smoking and to help health-care professionals treat tobacco use and dependence.)

http://www.surgeongeneral.gov/tobacco/

U.S. Environmental Protection Agency

(This website offers information on the dangers of secondhand smoke.)

Ariel Rios Building

1200 Pennsylvania Avenue, N.W.

Washington, D.C. 20460

(866) SMOKE-FREE (for Smoke-free Homes Pledge)

http://www.epa.gov/smokefree

Appendix 3

Tobacco Cessation Resources

National Network of Tobacco Cessation Quitlines

These toll-free numbers provide a single access point to the National Network of Tobacco Cessation Quitlines. Callers are automatically routed to a state-run quitline, if one exists in their area. If there is no state-run quitline, callers are routed to the National Cancer Institute Quitline.

(800) QUITNOW (800-784-8669)

(800) 332-8615 (TTY)

National Cancer Institute's LiveHelp service

Callers within the United States with cancer- or tobacco-related questions can speak with National Cancer Institute specialists on the group's LiveHelp information line. Smoking cessation help is also available. Check the website for times that specialists are manning the phones.

(800) 4-CANCER (800-422-6237)

http://www.smokefree.gov/talk.html

QuitNet

QuitNet is a free Web service for smokers and ex-smokers to fight tobacco addiction. More than just a support system, the "Q" is an online community, where someone is always there to listen and help – twenty-four hours a day/seven days a week. However, some services require a membership fee.

http://www.quitnet.com

QuitNet Directory of Smoking-Cessation Programs

QuitNet maintains the largest database of local quit-smoking programs (U.S. only at this time). Search for programs near you by state or ZIP code.

www.quitnet.com/library/programs

Freedom From Smoking® Online (American Lung Association)

Access the American Lung Association's free online smoking-cessation program.

http://www.lungusa.org

WebMD Smoking Cessation Support Group

People share their personal experiences with others trying to quit smoking on this popular website.

http://boards.webmd.com/roundtable_topic/48

Nicotine Anonymous

Nicotine Anonymous is a nonprofit 12-step program where people help each other live nicotine-free lives. The program adapts the 12-step method from Alcoholics Anonymous.

http://www.nicotine-anonymous.org

QuitSmokeless.org™

This website is targeted specifically for those who wish to quit using smokeless tobacco.

http://www.quitsmokeless.org

Appendix 4

References

Prochaska JO, DiClemente CC, and Norcross JC. In search of how people change: Applications to addictive behaviors. *American Psychologist*, 47(9): 1102-1114, 1992.

Rose JE, Brauer LH, Behm FM, Cramblett M, Calkins K, and Lawhon D. Psychopharmacologic interactions between nicotine and ethanol. *Nicotine and Tobacco Research*, 1:133-144, 2004.

Shiffman S. Relapse following smoking cessation: A situational analysis. *Journal of Consulting and Clinical Psychology*, 50: 71-86, 1986.

Tindle HA, Rigotti NA, Davis RB, Barbeau EM, Kawachi I, and Shiffman S. Cessation among smokers of "light" cigarettes: Results from the 2000 National Health Interview Survey. *American Journal of Public Health*, 96: 1498-1504, August 2006.

Index

About the Illustrations

Lead illustrator Joe Kanasz graduated in 1983 from the Cleveland Institute of Art with a Bachelor of Fine Arts in Medical Illustration. He began his career at Case Western Reserve University and eventually landed at the Cleveland Clinic. Since 1985 he has been creating anatomical and surgical illustrations for lectures, journals, and medical books. He has been a professional member of the Association of Medical Illustrators (AMI) since 1993. In 2006 the AMI recognized him and the Cleveland Clinic medical illustration department with its Medical Book Award for illustrating the comprehensive atlas *Operative Urology at the Cleveland Clinic*. Joe is also an accomplished freelance illustrator of numerous books and publications, including *The Foot: Examination & Diagnosis*, *Plastic Surgery: Indications, Operations, and Outcomes*, and *Anatomic Basis of Neurologic Diagnosis*.

Cleveland Clinic Press

Cleveland Clinic Press is a full-line publisher of nonfiction trade books and other media for the medical, health, nutrition, cookbook, and exercise markets.

It is the mission of the Press to increase the health literacy of the American public and to dispel myths and misinformation about medicine, health care, and treatment. Our authors include leading authorities from Cleveland Clinic as well as a diverse list of experts drawn from medical and health institutions whose research and treatment breakthroughs have helped countless people.

Each Cleveland Clinic Guide provides the health-care consumer with practical, useful, reliable, and authoritative information of the the highest quality. Every book is reviewed for accuracy and timeliness by the experts of Cleveland Clinic.

www.clevelandclinicpress.org

Cleveland Clinic

Cleveland Clinic, located in Cleveland, Ohio, is a not-for-profit multispecialty academic medical center that integrates clinical and hospital care with research and education. Cleveland Clinic was founded in 1921 by four renowned physicians with a vision of providing outstanding patient care based upon the principles of cooperation, compassion, and innovation. *U.S. News & World Report* consistently names Cleveland Clinic as one of the nation's best hospitals in its annual "America's Best Hospitals" survey. Approximately 1,500 full-time salaried physicians at Cleveland Clinic and Cleveland Clinic Florida represent more than 120 medical specialties and subspecialties. In 2006, patients came for treatment from every state and 100 countries.

www.clevelandclinic.org